50 WALKS IN Sussex

50 WALKS OF 2–10 MILES

First published 2001
Researched and written by Nick Channer
Field-checked and updated 2007 by Nick Channer, David Hancock and Tim Locke

Series Management: Bookwork Creative Associates
Series Editors: Sandy Draper and Marilynne Lanng
Designers: Elizabeth Baldin and Andrew Milne
Picture Research: Vivien Little
Proofreaders: Suzanne Juby and Pamela Stagg
Cartography provided by the Mapping Services Department of AA Publishing

Produced by AA Publishing

Published by … its Limited,
whose regis… 4EA;
registered n…

A03370

ISBN: 978-0-7495-5601-3

A CIP catalogue record for this book is available from the British Library.

The contents of this book are believed correct at the time of printing. Nevertheless, the publishers cannot be held responsible for any errors or omissions or for changes in the details given in this book or for the consequences of any reliance on the information it provides. This does not affect your statutory rights. We have tried to ensure accuracy in this book, but things do change and we would be grateful if readers would advise us of any inaccuracies they may encounter.

We have taken all reasonable steps to ensure that these walks are safe and achievable by walkers with a realistic level of fitness. However, all outdoor activities involve a degree of risk and the publishers accept no responsibility for any injuries caused to readers whilst following these walks. For more advice on walking safely see page 144. The mileage range shown on the front cover is for guidance only – some walks may be less than or exceed these distances.

Visit AA Publishing's website www.theAA.com/travel

Colour reproduction by Keenes Group, Andover
Printed by Printer Trento Srl, Italy

Acknowledgements
The Automobile Association would like to thank the following photographers, companies and picture libraries for their assistance in the preparation of this book.

3 AA/J Miller; 9 AA/M Busselle; 13 AA/J Miller; 14 AA/J Miller; 39 AA/J Miller;
40 AA/AM Busselle; 62/63 AA/J Miller; 82/83 AA/J Miller; 99 AA/P Brown; 100 AA/J Miller;
110/111 AA/J Miller; 133 AA/J Miller; 134 AA/J Miller

Every effort has been made to trace the copyright holders, and we apologise in advance for any accidental errors. We would be happy to apply corrections in following editions of this publication.

Right: Wheat fields near Ditchling (Walk 23)

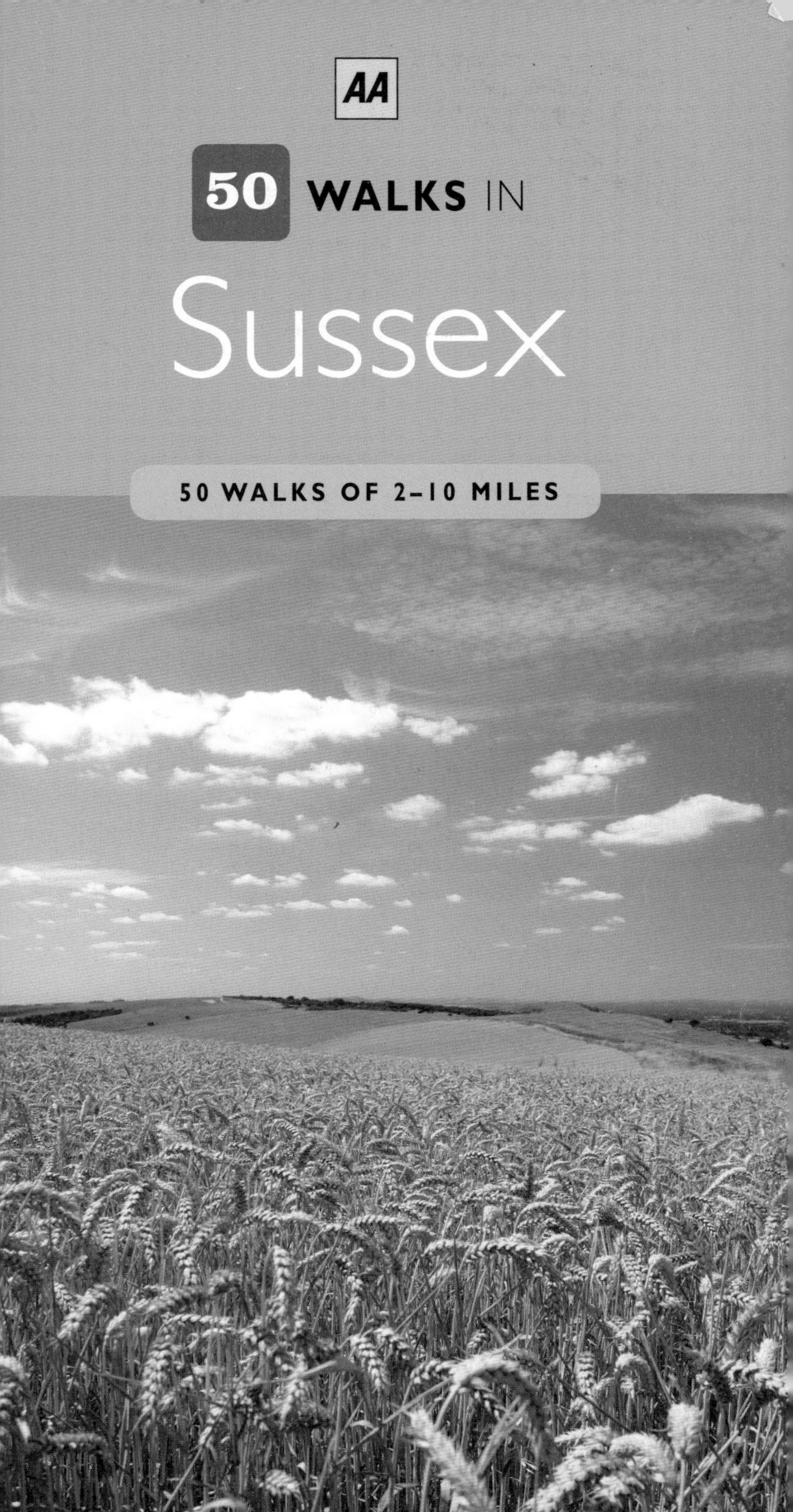
AA
50 WALKS IN
Sussex
50 WALKS OF 2–10 MILES

Contents

Contents

Rating
Each walk is rated for its relative difficulty compared to the other walks in this book. Walks marked ✚✚✚ are likely to be shorter and easier with little total ascent. The hardest walks are marked ✚✚✚

Walking in Safety
For advice and safety tips see page 144.

Locator Map

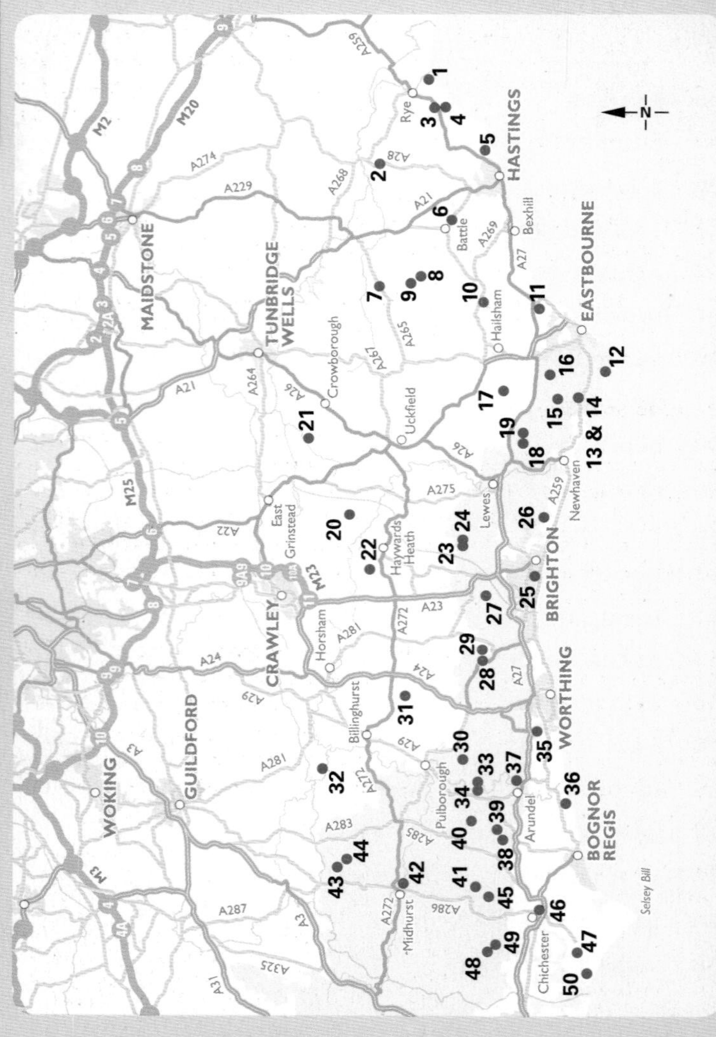

Legend

(dashed line with arrow)	Walk Route		Built-up Area
1	Route Waypoint		Woodland Area
(dashed line)	Adjoining Path		Toilet
	Viewpoint	P	Car Park
•	Place of Interest		Picnic Area
	Steep Section	)(	Bridge

Introducing Sussex

Divided into East and West Sussex, back in 1888 for administrative purposes, Sussex is so typically English that to walk through its landscape will feel like a walk through the whole country. Within its boundaries lies a wide variety of landscape and coastal scenery, but it is the spacious and open South Downs with which Sussex is most closely associated.

This swathe of breezy downland represents some of the finest walking in southern England – an oasis of green in the midst of encroaching urban development. Designated an Area of Outstanding Natural Beauty and ear-marked for full National Park status, the 90-mile (144km) chain of the Downs provide locals, as well as the many visitors, with a perfect natural playground. Kite flyers, model-aircraft enthusiasts, cyclists and hang-gliders are among the crowds who flock to these windswept chalk uplands.

Inspirational Sussex

But it is walkers who are probably most at home here. Wooded in the west and bare and exposed in the east, the Downs offer miles of exhilarating walking. A bracing hike along the ridge of these hills is often accompanied by the faint tang of the sea and magnificent views of the coast and the Weald. The writer Hilaire Belloc regarded the South Downs as a national institution which lifted people's experience and understanding of them to something approaching a religious creed. He wrote of Sussex as if it were the 'crown of England'.

Another writer whose love affair with Sussex lasted a lifetime was Rudyard Kipling. Perhaps the best way to see his 'blunt, bow-headed, whale-backed Downs' is from the South Downs Way which runs like a thread across the ridge of the hills and is one of Britain's most popular long distance trails. However, the South Downs can be seen and admired from countless vantage points and for anyone who loves and appreciates the English landscape, a glimpse of a dramatic downland escarpment against the sky leaves a lasting impression.

Sussex Landscapes

While some of the best walking will be found on the South Downs, there are many opportunities to explore the rest of Sussex on foot. The walks in this guide reach every corner of the county, from the gentle coastal terrain of Chichester Harbour to the glorious wooded landscape of Ashdown Forest.

The routes are designed to capture the essence and spirit of Sussex, visiting many of its famous landmarks and revealing the diversity of its splendid scenery. Every aspect of its history and geology is recorded. All that has shaped and influenced this county over the centuries is here.

PUBLIC TRANSPORT

Sussex is well served by public transport, making many of the walks in this guide easily accessible. The Winchelsea, Battle, Pevensey, Arlington, Horsted Keynes, Brighton, Amberley, Arundel and Chichester walks (routes 3/4, 6, 11, 17, 21, 26, 33/34, 37 and 46) start at a railway station or near to it. For times of trains throughout Sussex call the 24-hour national train inquiry line on 08457 48 49 50; www.nationalrail.co.uk or Journeycall on 0871 200 3456; www.journeycall.com. For bus times call 0871 200 2233; www.traveline.org.uk. For countrywide public transport information look at the internet site www.pti.org.uk.

Walking in Sussex

It may be something of a cliché but walking remains our most popular outdoor activity. There is little to add to this statistic, save to say that one of its greatest pleasures is the opportunity to learn so much more about the countryside. A really good walk should be educational, enjoyable and informative, providing a unique insight into the changing character of our rural landscape.

Each route in this book offers a specific theme to enhance the walk, as well as lots of snippets of useful information on what to look for and what to do while you're there. The majority of the walks are circular and almost all are rural rambles, but if you like a city stroll, there are town walks in historic Chichester and vibrant Brighton. Above all, take your time and enjoy the many delights that Sussex offers the explorer on foot.

Waymarks in Sussex

On your walks around Sussex, you will see various waymarking signs: blue arrows indicate bridleways, suitable for walkers, cyclists and horse-riders; yellow arrows indicate footpaths, suitable for walkers only; red arrows indicate byways, open to all traffic; and acorn markers indicate National Trails, such as the South Downs Way, and the Cleveland Way.

Using this book

INFORMATION PANELS

An information panel for each walk shows its relative difficulty (see page 5), the distance and total amount of ascent. An indication of the gradients you will encounter is shown by the rating ▲▲▲ (no steep slopes) to ▲▲▲ (several very steep slopes).

MAPS

There are 30 maps, covering 40 of the walks. Some walks have a suggested option in the same area. The information panel for these walks will tell you how much extra walking is involved. On short-cut suggestions the panel will tell you the total distance if you set out from the start of the main walk. Where an option returns to the same point on the main walk, just the distance of the loop is given. Where an option leaves the main walk at one point and returns to it at another, then the distance shown is for the whole walk. The minimum time suggested is for reasonably fit walkers and doesn't allow for stops. Each walk has a suggested Ordnance Survey map.

START POINTS

The start of each walk is given as a six-figure grid reference prefixed by two letters indicating which 100-km square of the National Grid it refers to. You'll find more information on grid references on most Ordnance Survey maps.

DOGS

We have tried to give dog owners useful advice about how dog friendly each walk is. Please respect other countryside users. Keep your dog under control, especially around livestock, and obey local bylaws and other dog control notices.

CAR PARKING

Many of the car parks suggested are public, but occasionally you may find you have to park on the roadside or in a lay-by. Please be considerate when you leave your car, ensuring that access roads or gates are not blocked and that other vehicles can pass safely.

Right: South Downs near Alfriston (Walk 15)

How Rye Repelled the Enemy

Wide skies, lonely seas and lagoons form the backdrop to this remote coastal walk, which is excellent for birding.

DISTANCE *4.5 miles (7.2km)* MINIMUM TIME *2hrs*

ASCENT/GRADIENT *Negligible* ▲▲▲ LEVEL OF DIFFICULTY +++

PATHS *Level paths and good, clear tracks, no stiles*

LANDSCAPE *Mixture of shingle expanses and old gravel workings, now part of a local nature reserve*

SUGGESTED MAP *OS Explorer 125 Romney Marsh, Rye & Winchelsea*

START / FINISH *Grid reference: TQ 942189*

DOG FRIENDLINESS *Dogs on lead within Rye Harbour Local Nature Reserve*

PARKING *Spacious free car park at Rye Harbour*

PUBLIC TOILETS *Rye Harbour*

Turn the clock back to the dark days of the Second World War and you would find Rye Harbour a very different place. Blockhouses for machine guns littered the coast and barbed wire and landmines made it a 'no go' area. During the hours of darkness great searchlights swept across the night sky; they were particularly effective at detecting the dreaded flying bombs. Go there now and you can still identify some of these crumbling relics of war. It's a fascinating exercise to rewrite the pages of history and imagine what might have happened if enemy forces had landed on this forgotten corner of England.

Napoleonic Threat

But this wasn't the first time the area had been under threat. During the Napoleonic Wars, 150 years earlier, Rye Harbour was considered an obvious target for invasion and attack when the Martello tower, seen by the car park at the start of the walk, became the first of 47 fortifications built in Sussex as a defence against the French. The tower would certainly have been a tough deterrent. The walls are nearly 12ft (4m) thick at the base and the middle floor would have been occupied by a garrison of one officer and 24 men.

Since then, the sea has built up over half a mile (800m) of land in front of it, with violent storms dumping huge deposits of shingle on the shore every winter. Today, the little community of Rye Harbour is peaceful and yet, years after the shadows of war have passed over, it still conveys that same sense of bleak isolation. Though not as atmospheric as neighbouring, shingle-strewn Dungeness, it does feel very isolated here.

Part of a designated Site of Special Scientific Interest (SSSI), Rye Harbour Local Nature Reserve lies at the mouth of the River Rother, which forms its eastern boundary. During its early stages, the walk follows the river and at first glance the shingle seems so bare and inhospitable that it is hard to imagine any plant could grow here. But in late May and June the beach is transformed by a colourful array of flowers. Delicate yellow horned poppies, sea kale, carpets of seaweed and countless other species of plants thrive in this habitat. Salt marsh, vegetation along the river's edge, pools and grazing marsh add to the variety and the old gravel pits now represent an important site for nesting terns, gulls, ducks and waders. Rye Harbour is best known for its superb bird life and is always very popular with ornithologists.

The walk follows the coast for some time, passing the Ternery Pool, originally two separate gravel workings dug by hand early in the 20th century. It continues along the coast before heading inland to some more flooded gravel pits. Here you might easily spot gulls, grebes, cormorants, swallows and reed warblers. Turtle doves are often seen in the fields and sometimes perch in pairs on the overhead wires.

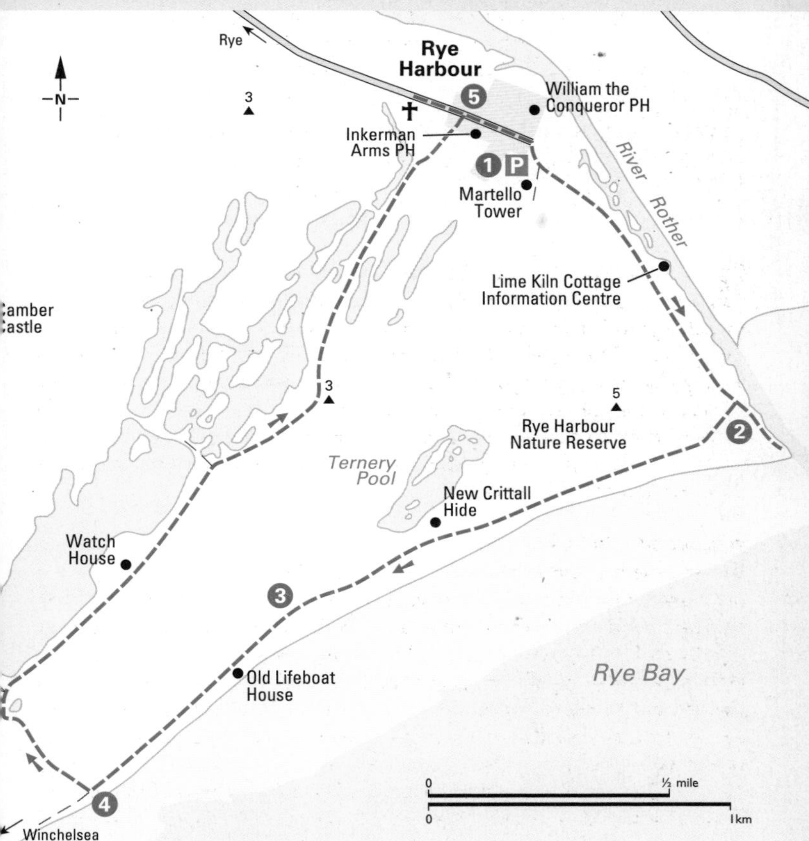

WALK 1 DIRECTIONS

1 Keep the Martello Tower and the entrance to the holiday village on your right and enter Rye Harbour Local Nature Reserve. The Rother can be seen on the left, running parallel to the path. Head for Lime Kiln Cottage information centre and continue on the firm path, with the Rother still visible on the left. The sprawling expanse of Camber Sands, a popular holiday destination, nudges into view beyond the river mouth.

❷ Follow the path to the beach, then retrace your steps to the point where a permissive path runs off to the left, cutting between wildlife sanctuary areas where access is not allowed. Pass the entrance to the New Crittall hide on the right. From here there are superb views over Ternery Pool. In the distance, Rye's jumble of houses can be seen sprawling over the hill. Continue west on the clear path and gradually it edges nearer the shore.

WHAT TO LOOK FOR

The little tern is one of Rye Harbour's summer visitors. Arriving in April, it stays until September when it departs for its wintering grounds on the African coast. Several eggs are laid in May on bare shingle or sand along the coast. The best colonies are found in protected areas controlled by wardens. Through their efforts, the populations of these terns have increased in recent years.

❸ Ahead now is the outline of the old abandoned lifeboat house and, away to the right in the distance, the unmistakable profile of Camber Castle. Keep going on the clear path until you reach a waymarked footpath on the right, running towards a line of houses on the eastern edge of Winchelsea.

WHERE TO EAT AND DRINK

The Inkerman Arms at Rye Harbour specialises in seafood and locally caught fresh fish. Food is available both at lunchtime and in the evening. Also in Rye Harbour, the William the Conqueror pub serves food and nearby Bosun's Bite café offers a range of sandwiches, baguettes and burgers.

❹ Take this footpath and head inland, passing a small pond on the right. Glancing back, the old lifeboat house can be seen standing out starkly against the sky. Turn right at the next junction, pass the Watch House and continue on the track as it runs alongside several lakes. Pass to the left of some dilapidated farm outbuildings and keep going along the track. The lakes are still seen on the left-hand side, dotted with trees, and the silent, motionless figures of fishermen can often be seen along here. Begin the approach to Rye Harbour and on the left is the spire of the church.

❺ On reaching the road in the centre of the village of Rye, turn left to visit the fascinating parish church before heading back along the main street. Pass the Inkerman Arms and return to the car park at the start of the walk.

WHILE YOU'RE THERE

Stop and look at the old lifeboat station beside the route of the walk. It's not been used since one stormy night in November 1928 when the 17-strong crew of the *Mary Stanford* were called to rescue a leaking steamer in the English Channel. The volunteers ran from their beds and dragged the lifeboat into the sea through gale force winds and huge waves. Soon afterwards, the coastguard heard the steamer was safe but with no ship-to-shore radio available he was unable to convey a message to the lifeboat crew. The next day, the *Mary Stanford* was seen floating upside down in the water. Not one volunteer survived the tragedy. Today the old building lies empty, abandoned and forlorn – in keeping with its surroundings. The churchyard at Rye Harbour has a memorial to the crew of the *Mary Stanford*.

Right: Boats in the harbour at Rye (Walk 1)

RX168

Great Dixter and its Glorious Gardens

A pleasant walk on the Sussex/Kent border, highlighting the skill and creativity of a famous architect and a gifted gardening writer.

DISTANCE *3 miles (4.8km)* MINIMUM TIME *1hr 30min*

ASCENT/GRADIENT *98ft (30m)* ▲▲▲ LEVEL OF DIFFICULTY +++

PATHS *Field paths and quiet roads, 8 stiles*

LANDSCAPE *Undulating farmland and stretches of woodland*

SUGGESTED MAP *OS Explorer 125 Romney Marsh, Rye & Winchelsea*

START / FINISH *Grid reference: TQ 828245*

DOG FRIENDLINESS *Dog stiles near Great Dixter and on Sussex Border Path*

PARKING *Free car park on corner of Fullers Lane and A28, Northiam*

PUBLIC TOILETS *Great Dixter, seasonal opening*

Deep in the tranquil, rolling countryside of East Sussex, close to the Kent border, lies the wonderful Great Dixter, one of the county's smaller and more intimate historic houses.

Family Theme

Built in the middle of the 15th century and later restored and enlarged by Sir Edwin Lutyens, Great Dixter is a popular tourist attraction as well as a family home. These days this fine Wealden hall-house is owned and cared for by Olivia Eller and was the home of her late uncle, Christopher Lloyd, the gardening writer, who died in 2006. It was Christopher's father, Nathaniel, who instructed Lutyens in 1910 to make major changes to Great Dixter, which at that time was in a poor state of repair. His main task was to clear the house of later alterations and, typically, the work was undertaken with great sensitivity.

But Lutyens didn't stop there. While all the restoration plans were beginning to take shape he and Nathaniel Lloyd seized on the opportunity to improve and enlarge the house. A complete timber-framed yeoman's hall at Benenden in Kent, scheduled for demolition, was skilfully dismantled and moved to Great Dixter, adding an entire wing to the house.

One of Great Dixter's most striking features is the magnificent Great Hall, the largest surviving timber-framed hall in the country. Visitors never fail to be impressed by its medieval splendour. The half-timbered and plastered front and the Tudor porch also catch the eye. The contents of Great Dixter date mainly from the 17th and 18th centuries and were collected over the years by Nathaniel Lloyd. The house also contains many examples of delicately fashioned needlework, which were completed by his wife Daisy and their children.

Impressive Gardens

However, a tour of Great Dixter doesn't end with the house. The gardens are equally impressive. Christopher Lloyd spent many years working on this project, incorporating many medieval buildings, establishing natural

Left: The cottage garden in Great Dixter (Walk 2)

ponds and designing yew topiary. The result is one of the most exciting, colourful and constantly changing gardens of modern times.

As with the house, plans were drawn up to improve the gardens, and here Lutyens was just as inventive. He often used tiles in a decorative though practical manner, to great effect. At Great Dixter he took a chicken house with crumbling walls and transformed it into an open-sided loggia, supported by laminated tile pillars.

Beginning in Northiam, the walk heads round the edge of the village before reaching the house at Great Dixter. Even out of season, when the place is closed, you gain a vivid impression of the house and its Sussex Weald setting. Passing directly in front of Great Dixter, the route then crosses rolling countryside to join the Sussex Border Path, following it all the way back to Northiam.

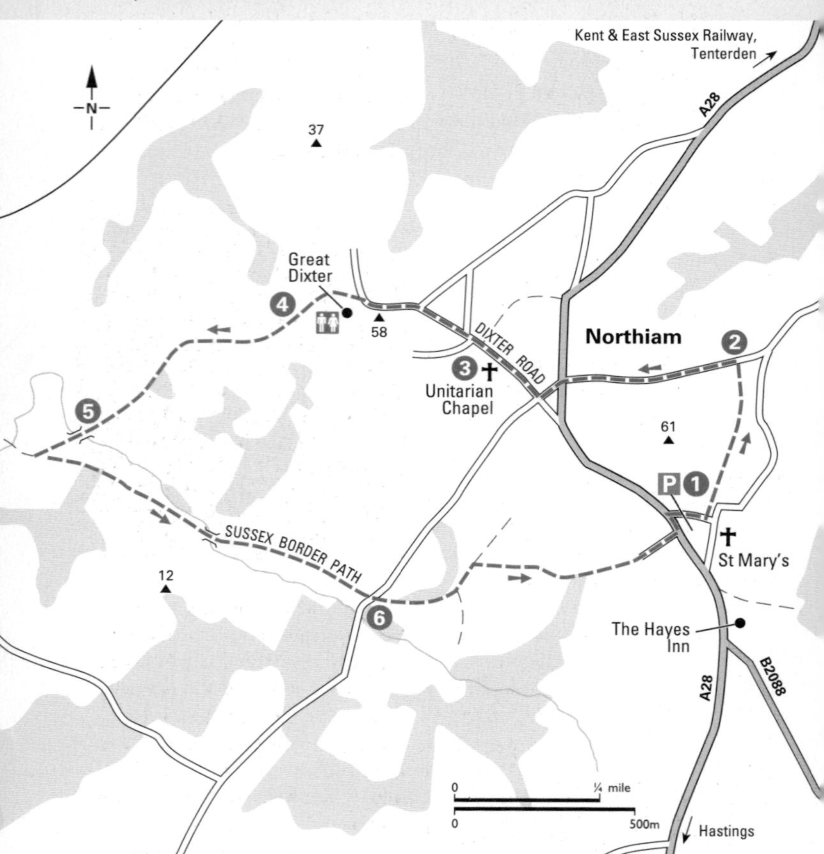

WALK 2 DIRECTIONS

❶ Turn right out of the car park and walk along Fullers Lane towards St Mary's Church. Take the path on the left, signposted to Goddens Gill, and keep to the right edge of the field. Go through a gate in the corner and look for an oasthouse on the right. Make for a path on the far side of the field and follow it between fences towards a thatched cottage. Go through a gate to the road.

WHILE YOU'RE THERE

Travel a mile (1.6km) or so along the A28 to take a train ride on the delightful Kent and East Sussex Railway. The railway, which opened in 1900, ran from Robertsbridge to Headcorn and was used mainly for taking farm produce to market, and for bringing in coal to drive machinery and for household fires. The coal yard at the station is still in use. The line closed to passengers in 1954 and to goods in 1961. Northiam station reopened in 1990 through the efforts of the *Challenge Anneka* television show.

2 Turn left and head for the A28. Bear diagonally left across the A28 and follow Thyssel Lane signposted 'Great Dixter'. Turn right at the crossroads, following Dixter Road.

3 Pass the Unitarian Chapel and avoid the path on the right. Pass Higham Lane on the left and continue to follow the signs for Great Dixter. Disregard a turning on the right (Dixter Lane) and go straight on, following a path between trees and hedges, parallel to the main drive to the house.

WHERE TO EAT AND DRINK

The Hayes Inn at Northiam is open all day and serves bar food. Alternatively, Pat-a-cake Bakery has a tea room. When Great Dixter is open, you can buy soft drinks and basic prepacked snacks from the gift shop. There is also a picnic area.

4 Pass the toilets and head towards a cattle grid. Cross the stile just to the left of it and follow the path signposted to Ewhurst. Follow the waymarks and keep the hedge on the left. Cross a stile in the field corner and then head diagonally down the field slope to the next stile. Follow the clear path down the field slope.

5 Make for a footbridge and then turn left to join the Sussex Border Path. The path skirts the field before disappearing left into some woodland. Emerging from the trees, cut straight across the next field to two stiles and a footbridge. Keep the woodland on the left and look for a gap in the trees. Cross a stream to a stile and bear right. Follow the right edge of the field and keep on the Sussex Border Path until you reach the road.

WHAT TO LOOK FOR

Walk briefly off the route to visit Northiam's parish church. Not much is known of its early history, though part of it dates from the 12th century. Most of the chancel is modern. Have a look at the clock which was repaired and restored through the generosity of parishioners. A victory peel of bells rang out on 8th May 1945 – VE Day – and the names of the six bell ringers are recorded inside the church.

6 Cross over the lane to a drive. Bear immediately left and follow the path to a stile. Pass alongside woodland and then veer slightly away from the trees to a stile in the approaching boundary. Cross it and go straight ahead up the field slope. Take the first footpath on the right and follow it to a gap in the field corner. Cross a footbridge under the trees and continue along the right-hand edge of the next field to join a drive. Bear left and follow it to the A28. Cross over to return to the car park at Northiam.

WALK 3

Stranded Winchelsea – Abandoned by the Sea

Explore a Cinque Port with a record of bad luck before following an historic line of defence.

DISTANCE *4.5 miles (7.2km)* **MINIMUM TIME** *2hrs*

ASCENT/GRADIENT *197ft (60m)* ▲▲▲ **LEVEL OF DIFFICULTY** +++

PATHS *Field paths and pavements, 15 stiles*

LANDSCAPE *Mixture of marshland and undulating farmland*

SUGGESTED MAP *OS Explorer 124 Hastings & Bexhill or 125 Romney Marsh, Rye & Winchelsea*

START / FINISH *Grid reference: TQ 905173*

DOG FRIENDLINESS *On lead near birding hide and across farmland*

PARKING *Roadside parking near St Thomas's Church at Winchelsea*

PUBLIC TOILETS *Winchelsea*

The story of Winchelsea is fascinating. Extraordinarily unlucky, surely nowhere else in the country can have fallen victim to fate in quite the same way. Looking at the sleepy town today, it seems hard to believe it was once a thriving port, one of the most important on the south coast.

Cinque Port

This delightful little town, one of the seven Cinque Ports and characterised by elegant houses and quiet, grid pattern streets, became stranded when the sea receded, exposing a stretch of fertile marshland. Now it lies more than a mile (1.6km) inland. But Winchelsea's run of bad luck did not begin and end with the vagaries of the ocean. The new town replaced Old Winchelsea in the late 13th century when it was inundated by the sea and swept away by a great storm in 1287. The old town now lies beneath the English Channel, somewhere out in Rye Bay. As the water encroached, the inhabitants built new homes on the hilltop, establishing themselves on higher ground before the disaster finally took hold.

A Planner's Dream

The new town was conceived and sited personally by King Edward I, and, with its regular grid pattern, has long been acknowledged as perhaps the first example of medieval English town planning. Only a dozen of the proposed 39 grid squares were ever completed and the ambitious plans for the new Winchelsea were eventually abandoned. Three gates, part of the original fortification, still survive, including Strand Gate with its four round towers. Many of the buildings you see in the town today date back only about 100 years.

The town's bad luck continued through the Middle Ages when Winchelsea came under constant attack from the French and suffered heavy damage. The church, much of which was destroyed during the last raid of 1449, includes the tomb of Gervase Alard, England's first admiral, as well as various monuments and a wall painting from the 14th century.

WINCHELSEA

WALK 3

Before starting the walk, take a leisurely tour round the town. It's well worth the effort and the views from Strand Gate out towards the Channel are very impressive. This is a walk of two extremes. From Winchelsea's lofty vantage point, you'll descend to a bare, rather featureless landscape, skirting a flat expanse of water-meadows known as Pett Level. The return leg is more undulating, with good views both of the coast and Winchelsea's unspoiled hilltop setting.

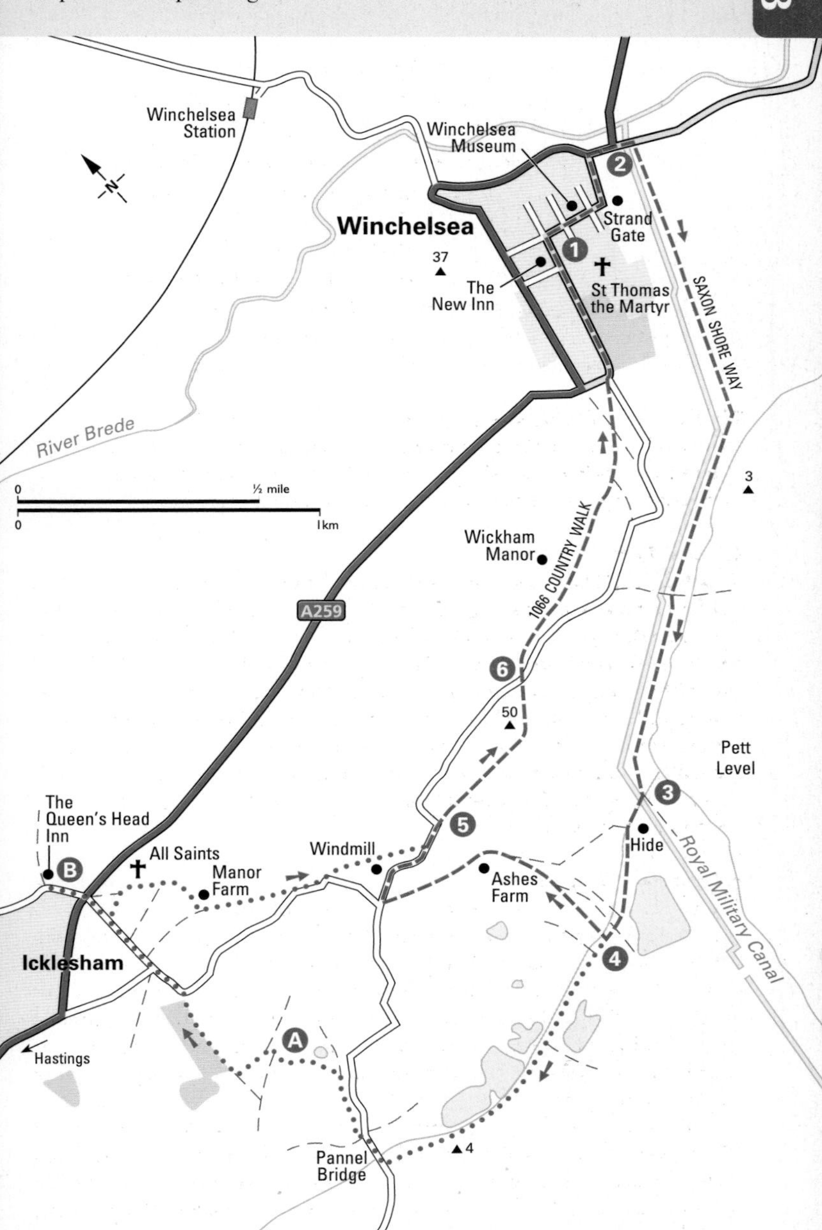

WALK 3 DIRECTIONS

1 With The New Inn on your left and ruined St Thomas's church on the right, follow the road round the right-hand bend. Head down to Strand Gate and then take the road to the junction with the A259. Turn right and follow the pavement along here.

2 When the road bends left, turn right at the sign for Winchelsea Beach. Cross the Royal Military Canal and bear immediately right. Follow the tow path across this empty landscape. Cross a stile and avoid a concrete footbridge. Eventually, the canal begins to curve left. There's a stile and galvanised gate here.

3 Bear right for a few paces beyond it at the footbridge. Cross a second wooden footbridge over a ditch and make for a gate. Pass the birding hide and continue along the path, making for the next footbridge.

4 Turn right here, veer right and then follow the path as it curves left through the reedbeds. Begin a moderate climb and head towards a house. Keep to the left of it and follow the path through the trees. Bear right at gates up some steps to a stile, turn left along the field-edge to another stile. Cross a drive, go through a gate and go straight across the field to a stile, then bear right for a few paces to two more stiles. Skirt the field to the next stile and exit to the road. Keep right here, signposted 'Winchelsea', and soon you pass below the hilltop windmill, avoiding the 1066 Country Walk which meets the road at this point.

WHILE YOU'RE THERE

Visit the Winchelsea Museum, which highlights over 700 years of the Cinque Port's history. Models, maps, pictures, artefacts and memorabilia illustrate the history of the town. Call into the birding hide, part of the Pannel Valley Reserve. From here, you will probably be able to spot teals, coots, shelducks or geese on the water.

5 Go straight ahead over a stile when the lane bends left and cross the field. Look for a stile and keep alongside some trees to the next stile. Continue ahead, pass an old pill box and head down the gentle field slope to the road.

WHAT TO LOOK OUT FOR

The Royal Military Canal runs below Winchelsea and extends for 25 miles (40.5km). Constructed at the beginning of the 19th century, its purpose was to protect the exposed south-east coast from invasion by Napoleon's forces. William Cobbett mentions the canal in his *Rural Rides*, wondering how a 30-ft (9m) wide ditch could possibly deter troops who had managed to cross the Rhine and the Danube. The Saxon Shore Way follows the tow path.

6 Turn right for a few paces to a stile on the left. Bear right, still on the 1066 Country Walk, and cross the next stile. Keep to the right of Wickham Manor and look for a stile in the far boundary. Cross the drive to a stile and keep ahead across the fields. Make for a stile and gate in the bottom left corner and follow the 1066 Country Walk waymarks. The path veers over to the right to two stiles. Bear left and begin a moderate ascent to a stone stile. Turn right at the road, follow it round to the left and return to the centre of Winchelsea.

Winchelsea and Icklesham

A longer walk through the gentle Pannel Valley.
See map and information panel for Walk 3

DISTANCE *6.25 miles (10km)* MINIMUM TIME *3hrs*
ASCENT/GRADIENT *246ft (75m)* ▲▲▲ LEVEL OF DIFFICULTY +++
PATHS *Field paths and quiet roads, 16 stiles*
LANDSCAPE *Valley terrain and undulating farmland*

WALK 4 DIRECTIONS (Walk 3 option)

Keep walking ahead at Point 4 and follow the obvious path. Go across several stiles and, on reaching the road, turn right. Cross Pannel Bridge and just past the drive to Little Pannel Farm go up some steps. Bear right parallel with the road and take the second path left, soon to keep left of a pond and skirting a line of trees, Point A.

Make for a gap and veer left to a fork. Keep to the right and follow the path as it curves right, then ignore a right-hand path. Make for some dense woodland and keep left at the road.

Walk along Workhouse Lane to the village of Icklesham, crossing the busy A259 to reach The Queen's Head inn, Point B. From here retrace your steps back to Workhouse Lane, pass the village hall and then turn left to join the 1066 Country Walk. Pass Icklesham's All Saints Church, whose archives include detailed evacuation plans made in 1798 when this area was in imminent danger of invasion, and continue on the trail to Manor Farm.

Pass the outbuildings, continue ahead for a few paces at the junction and turn left at the gate. Follow the waymarked footpath through apple orchards, heading towards a privately owned windmill, and make for a gate leading out to the road. Turn left and, when the lane bends right after a few steps, cross the stile on the corner and continue along the 1066 Country Walk.

Follow the path up the grassy slope and keep to the left of the windmill, which was used by Paul McCartney as a recording studio. A glorious view of the Pannel Valley, the Royal Military Canal and the coast opens up in front of you. Drop down to a stile and some cottages and turn left at the road. Follow Walk 3 Points 5 and 6 back to Winchelsea.

WHERE TO EAT AND DRINK

The 18th-century New Inn at Winchelsea offers superb cask ales, traditional home-cooked food and a cosy restaurant in which to dine. There is also a popular beer garden for summer lunchtimes and warm evenings. The Queen's Head inn in Icklesham also offers traditional food, good ales and superb views towards Rye.

Ride Down to Hastings Old Town

Follow two long distance trails and travel by cliff railway on this spectacular coastal walk.

DISTANCE *4.5 miles (7.2km)* MINIMUM TIME *2hrs 30min*

ASCENT/GRADIENT *328ft (100m)* ▲▲▲ LEVEL OF DIFFICULTY +++

PATHS *Tracks, minor roads and coastal paths*

LANDSCAPE *High ground overlooking coast, with glens revealing layers of sandstone*

SUGGESTED MAP *OS Explorer 124 Hastings & Bexhill*

START / FINISH *Grid reference:TQ 847117*

DOG FRIENDLINESS *Return walk, along coast path, is ideal for dogs off lead*

PARKING *Fairlight Road free car park and picnic site*

PUBLIC TOILETS *At car park*

WALK 5 DIRECTIONS

It might be a bit off the beaten track, but the picnic site at Fairlight Road is definitely worth finding. Plenty of people come here simply to relax and picnic in warmer weather, but there are many others who use this location as the starting point for a walk into the surrounding countryside or along the glorious coast.

From the car park, go out to the road and then cross over to join the waymarked 1066 Country Walk. Follow the wide track down through the trees and turn right, avoiding a turning on the left to Fairlight Glen, and keep going along Barley Lane. Pass between the camping and caravan sites, ignoring a turning on the right that leads to Ore.

Follow the tarmac road and pass Barley Lane car park. Avoid a path to Harold Road and keep left at the fork, by the sign for Ecclesbourne Lodge. The sea begins to edge into view now and over to the right is a sprawling jumble of rooftops, with rows of terraced houses scattered over the slopes and hillsides. This is residential Hastings.

Pass the entrance to Rocklands Holiday Park and then cross the grassy expanse of East Hill by aiming slightly right. Hastings pier and much of the town can be seen down below you, creating an impressive picture. Keep the pier in your sights and follow the footpath across the broad, grassy expanse of East Hill.

Make for the East Hill cliff railway, the steepest in Britain, and take a ride down to Hastings Old Town. This is public transport at its best.

WHERE TO EAT AND DRINK

There is a restaurant at Underwater World and there is also a good choice of several good restaurants, cafés and pubs to suit most tastes in Hastings Old Town, including the Kings Head and the Crown.

WHAT TO LOOK OUT FOR

On East Hill above Hastings is a beacon, erected in 1988 to commemorate the 400th anniversary of the Spanish Armada. The original beacon was found at nearby North Seat. The hill also marks the site of an Iron Age settlement, established by Celts in about 40 BC. Defended by earth banks and the cliff face, the site occupied a prominent position overlooking a natural harbour.

The journey is simple, short and straightforward and the views are magnificent. Emerging into the street below, have a look at this quaint corner of the resort. With its timber, net shops, cliff railway and high-sterned fishing boats pulled up on the beach, Hastings Old Town is far removed in both character and appearance from the main town.

The Old Town lies in a valley with several fine churches, narrow old passageways and medieval houses. Steps lead up to cottages built into the hillside. Hemmed in by steep cliffs, the focal point of the Old Town is the High Street. It's not a large area, but there is always lots to see and plenty going on. The net shops, which stand near the boats, on the shingle beach known as the Stade, are not really shops at all but huts used for storing fishing nets and tackle. The huts, which are intentionally tall and narrow to reduce ground rent, are unique, being found only in Hastings.

Return to the cliff railway terminus and travel back up to East Hill. Swing right up some steps, avoiding the 1066 Country Walk, and follow the Saxon Shore Way along the southern slopes of East Hill, with the sea on your right. Pass a beacon on your left and keep to the right, eventually reaching a kissing gate and follow the sign right for Ecclesbourne Glen (lower).

Descend almost to sea level and then climb out of the glen via a flight of steps. On reaching a seat, turn left and follow the path as it heads briefly inland. Walk towards Fairlight Glen, following the signposts and the numbered bollards and when you reach bollard number ten, branch off left towards Barley Lane.

Ascend quite steeply between clumps of trees and bracken, making for bollard nine. Don't turn sharp left here, instead go through the kissing gate by the map of the area and follow the often wet and muddy path up to two gates. Cross the grass in front of some part tile-hung cottages and join a concrete farm track. Follow it left up to the road and cross over to the car park.

WHILE YOU'RE THERE

Make a point of visiting the Fishermen's Museum in Roc-a-Nore Road. It illustrates the history and tradition of fishing on this coast over the centuries. In the Middle Ages, Hastings was an important harbour and today fishing is still a major industry here. The town has the largest beach-launched fishing fleet in Europe. Underwater World in Hastings Old Town is well worth a visit too. Here you can walk through a glass tunnel beneath a spectacular 'reef pool' – home to sharks, rays, crabs and starfish. Visit the acre of subterranean tunnels and caverns at the Smugglers Adventure in Hastings Old Town and experience smuggling as it was over 200 years ago.

Battle – Britain's Most Famous Battlefield

Take a walk into history and visit the field where two men famously fought each other for the English crown.

DISTANCE *5 miles (8km)* **MINIMUM TIME** *2hrs 30min*

ASCENT/GRADIENT *448ft (140m)* ▲▲▲ **LEVEL OF DIFFICULTY** +++

PATHS *Field and woodland paths, some road walking, 10 stiles*

LANDSCAPE *Gently undulating farmland and woodland*

SUGGESTED MAP *OS Explorer 124 Hastings & Bexhill*

START / FINISH *Grid reference: TQ 747156*

DOG FRIENDLINESS *Enclosed woodland paths and stretches of 1066 Country Walk suitable for dogs off lead*

PARKING *Pay car park at Battle Abbey*

PUBLIC TOILETS *Mount Street car park in Battle, Brede Lane in Sedlescombe and Battle Abbey*

If one date from England's glorious past stands out more than any other, it is surely 1066. One of the most important and significant events of the last millennium, the Battle of Hastings represents a defining moment in British history.

Bloody Battle

Visit the battlefield and you can still sense something of that momentous day when William, Duke of Normandy, defeated Harold and his Saxon army and became William the Conqueror of England. See the spot where Harold is believed to have fallen and, by exercising a little imagination, you can picture the bloody events that led to his defeat.

William began by occupying a position on a hill about 400yds (365m) to the south of the English army, massed on a higher hilltop. Harold and his men fortified their formidable position and following abortive uphill charges on the English shield-wall, the Normans withdrew, unable to breach the defences. It looked for a time as if victory was within Harold's grasp until William rallied his men and executed two successful strategies. One was to instruct his bowmen to shoot their arrows indiscriminately into the air, though William had no idea that one of them would hit Harold in the eye, fatally wounding him. William's other plan was to create the impression that his armies were fleeing the battlefield. Sensing victory, the English gave chase but this was to be their downfall. The Normans rounded on them and won the battle. William marched victoriously to London where, on Christmas Day, in Westminster Abbey, he was duly crowned King of England.

William's Promise

Before the Battle of Hastings, William vowed that if God gave him victory that day, he would build an abbey on the site of the battle at Senlac Field. This he did, with the high altar set up on the spot where Harold died.

Little of the church remains today. The abbey, thought to have been completed before William died, was significantly enlarged and improved over the years that followed.

However, after the Dissolution of the Monasteries, much of it was converted into a private house by Sir Anthony Browne, Henry VIII's Master of Horse. Today, Battle Abbey is in the care of English Heritage and an immensely popular tourist attraction.

This attractive walk begins at Battle Abbey in the centre of picturesque Battle, which grew up around the abbey, so allow time before or after the walk to visit the abbey itself and its historic battlefield.

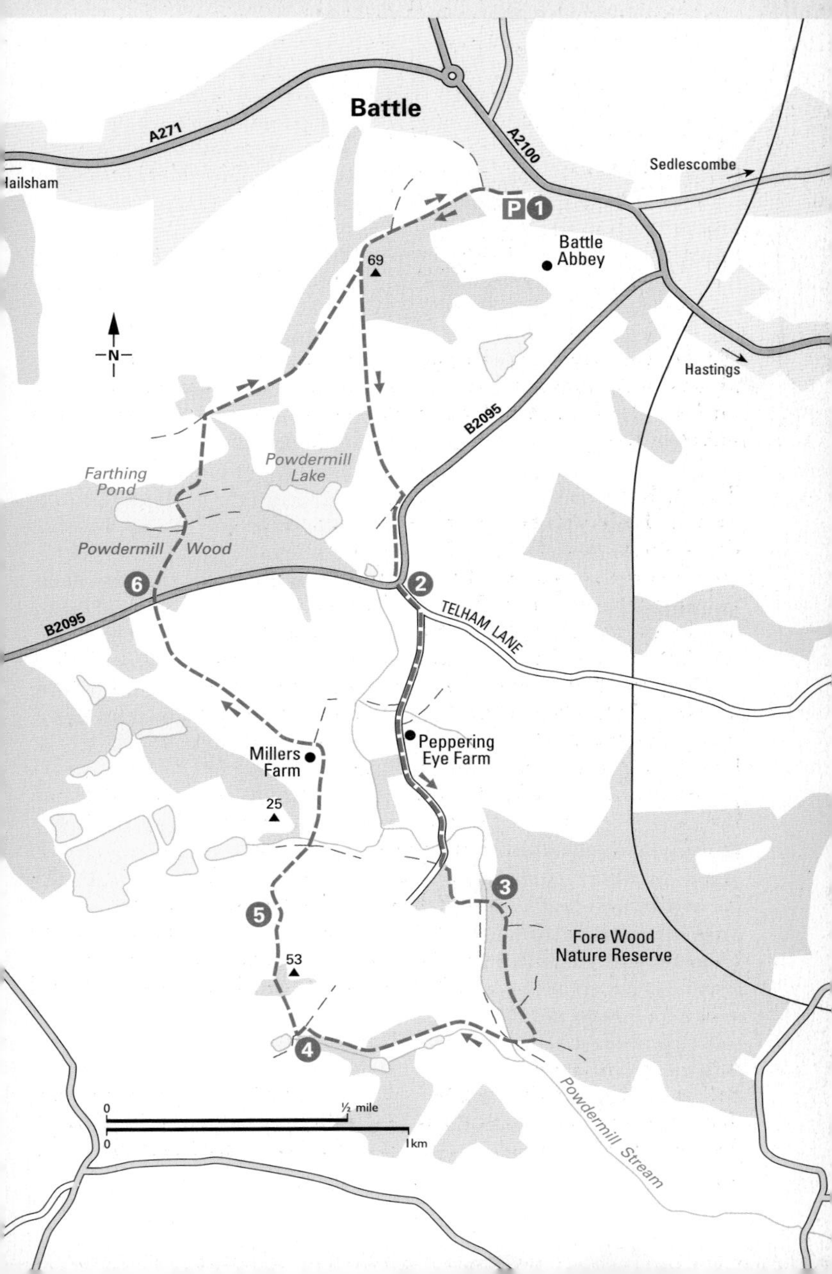

WALK 6 DIRECTIONS

❶ Turn left out of the car park and follow the track to a gate. Keep left along the bridleway beside woodland, the path swinging left to a fingerpost and junction of paths. Bear off left with the 1066 Bexhill Walk marker and walk down the field-edge and through two gates. Join a track and keep ahead, soon to cross a drive via stiles, and follow the fenced path along the field-edge high above the road to a stile.

❷ Cross the B2095 (take care – dangerous bend), walk along Telham Lane and take the Private Road right towards Peppering Eye Farm. Keep to the metalled drive for 0.5 mile (0.8km), passing Stumblet's Barn and crossing a stream to ascend to a junction of paths by Powdermill Cottage. Turn left along a track through the trees, drop downhill and bear off left with the waymarker across the centre of a field to cross a footbridge and enter Fore Wood (RSPB Nature Reserve).

WHAT TO LOOK OUT FOR

Fore Wood (RSPB Nature Reserve) is home to dragonflies, damselflies, nuthatches, treecreepers and woodpeckers, with rare mosses and ferns thriving in the shaded valleys.

❸ Bear right and follow the yellow-arrowed route through the edge of the wood, ignoring paths left and right, turning right where the path curves left at a bench. Go left at the fingerpost, cross a footbridge and follow the path right through scrub, parallel with the stream. On reaching an open field, keep left around the field-edge, pass a pond and gently climb along a defined path along the top edge of a field. The path becomes a track through trees, passing another larger pond, then soon emerges into a field, keeping ahead along the field-edge to a junction of tracks.

WHERE TO EAT AND DRINK

There are several pubs, restaurants and tea rooms in Battle, including the 15th-century Kings Head, the Pilgrims Rest tea room and the Almonry Coffee Shop. The Queens Head at Sedlescombe offers snacks, and the Clock House restaurant and tea room opposite serves Sussex cream teas.

❹ Bear left, then immediately right at a fork, curving left around a pond to reach a waymarker close to pheasant pens. Turn sharp right up the grassy bank, soon enter woodland and continue to a stile and footbridge. Turn left to another stile, then right along the field-edge passing a pond. Head across the field, pass beneath power cables and through a gate.

❺ Bear diagonally right downhill across the field to a gate and track. Just before some barns, climb the stile on the right to follow the arrowed path around Millers Farm to reach a gate. Rejoin the track and follow it out to a road.

❻ Cross the road, pass beside a gate and follow the path through Powdermill Wood. Cross the top end of Farthing Pond, bear sharp right and immediately fork off left, uphill along a narrow path through coppice woodland to a stile. Cross the field aiming to the right of a cottage to reach a stile. Turn right along a track, go through a gate and follow the 1066 Walk uphill through a field and soon retrace your outward route back to the car park.

Bateman's – Kipling's Good and Peaceable Place

Visit the National Trust home of one of Britain's most celebrated writers on this lovely walk in the Dudwell Valley.

DISTANCE *4.75 miles (7.7km)* **MINIMUM TIME** *2hrs*

ASCENT/GRADIENT *345ft (105m)* ▲▲▲ **LEVEL OF DIFFICULTY** +++

PATHS *Field and woodland paths, stretches of minor road, 12 stiles*

LANDSCAPE *Rolling, semi-wooded countryside of the Dudwell Valley*

SUGGESTED MAP *OS Explorers 124 Hastings & Bexhill, 136 The High Weald*

START / FINISH *Grid reference: TQ 674246 (on Explorer 136)*

DOG FRIENDLINESS *Dogs on lead in vicinity of Bateman's and Park Farm and on stretches of farmland. Off lead on woodland paths and tracks. Bateman's has a dog crêche*

PARKING *Free car park off A265 in Burwash village*

PUBLIC TOILETS *At car park*

Bateman's was Rudyard Kipling's refuge from the world. This was his spiritual home and it was here that he found true happiness. Touring the house and exploring the garden, it's not difficult to see why he fell in love with the place.

Kipling's Home

Bateman's is a charming family home, small and intimate, and occupying a peaceful setting in a secluded valley. Built by a local ironmaster in 1634, the house lies about 25 miles (40km) to the north-east of Kipling's old home at Rottingdean. Kipling purchased the house in 1902 and, now in the care of the National Trust, remains much as it was in Kipling's day.

It was here, in his book-lined study, that Kipling wrote some of his most famous works, including *Puck of Pook's Hill*. The house, and the peace and tranquillity of the surrounding countryside, greatly inspired him and over the years he acquired more and more land so that he could write and relax away from public scrutiny; 'We have loved it ever since our first sight of it', he wrote later.

Rose Garden

Kipling loved the garden just as much as the house, designing and landscaping it and putting his own mark on it. He planted yew hedges to give him more privacy and even erected a pear arch. Visitors to Bateman's can see the results of his labours and they can also take a stroll through the beautiful rose garden which he designed after being awarded the Nobel Prize for Literature in 1907.

Kipling was not a recluse and, although he relished his privacy, he liked to socialise but was known for his rather curious but discreet manner of asking guests to leave. He would lead them past the garden sundial, which indicated that it was later than it really was and hence suggest that they should make their farewells. He was a keen motorist too. He bought a

Rolls-Royce, which he maintained was the only car he could afford, and embarked on many journeys, travelling abroad and visiting his old school in Devon. He recorded his travels in detail and even dispatched reports and memos to the Automobile Association.

This glorious valley walk passes Bateman's near the start and then again towards the finish, enabling you to choose when you go there. A tour of the house and gardens reveals how the National Trust has preserved the character and integrity of the man, as well as the atmosphere of the place. Kipling died in 1936, after 34 years at Bateman's. Looking at the house today, it is not difficult to see why he described it as 'a real house in which to settle down for keeps...a good and peaceable place'.

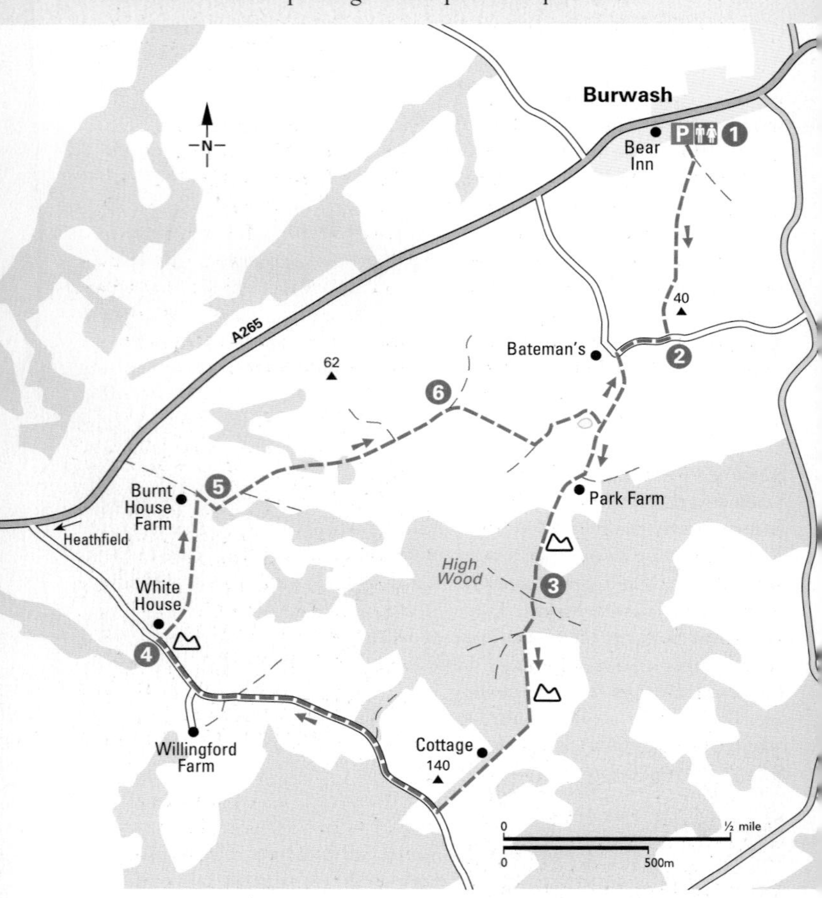

WALK 7 DIRECTIONS

1 Make for the footpath behind the toilet block. Follow the path down the slope and at a junction of paths cross the plank bridge and stile on the right. Continue ahead, making for the next stile and keep the boundary hedge on your right. Look for a stile on the right and then head diagonally down the field, keeping a fenced spinney on the right. Make for a stile in the field corner, follow the left-hand field-edge to the next stile, and exit to the road.

WHILE YOU'RE THERE

If you have time, make a point of visiting the watermill at Bateman's. The 18th-century mill, which was restored by dedicated volunteers, grinds corn for flour and attached to the wheel is one of the earliest water-driven turbines, installed by Rudyard Kipling to generate electricity for the house. There is a delightful walk from the house to the watermill on the River Dudwell.

2 Turn right and follow the lane along to Bateman's. Keep left in front of the house itself and make for Park Farm. Ignore the arrowed gate on the left, continue through the farm via two gates, then bear off left uphill through to the edge of some woodland to a gate. Head up the field slope, keeping the trees on your immediate right. Look for a gate and bridleway post on the right, passing through the wood to reach a track.

3 Bear left on the track, then immediately right and follow the bridleway, keeping left at the fork. Pass a solitary cottage and walk along to the road. Turn right, eventually to pass Willingford Farm and then start to climb quite steeply to reach a small white house on the right.

WHAT TO LOOK OUT FOR

Neighbouring Bateman's is the picturesque village of Burwash, which lies on a ridge between the rivers Rother and Dudwell. There are many white weatherboarded cottages and various beautiful tile-hung buildings, making it typical of East Sussex. The war memorial by the church was unveiled by Rudyard Kipling and his son is one of those commemorated. The church has a fine Norman tower with a shingled spire.

4 Go through a kissing gate and head straight along the top of the field. Make for a stile in the corner and head diagonally left in the next field; soon the buildings of Burnt House Farm come into view. Go through a small metal gate in the field corner, cross a paddock in front of the farm to a gate by some trees. Turn right along the field-edge to a kissing gate and go straight ahead in the next pasture, keeping a wrought-iron fence on your left.

5 Make for a gate ahead and cross the field by keeping to the left boundary. The path cuts across the next field to a stile. Pass through a belt of woodland to a field and head down to a stile by a gate. Follow a surfaced lane which very quickly becomes a grassy track, passing some dilapidated farm outbuildings.

WHERE TO EAT AND DRINK

The Bear Inn, next to the car park at Burwash, has been in business for more than 300 years. It serves bar meals, restaurant food and has a carvery on Sundays. The Bell Inn at Burwash is a delightful 17th-century inn with a log fire and a heavily beamed ceiling. Snacks and more substantial fare are available. Bateman's includes a popular tea room.

6 Cross over a stile by a gate and keep right here. Look for another stile after a few paces, turn left and then skirt round the edge of the field. Veer over to a stile towards the far end, cross a footbridge and turn left. Follow the path along to a pond, turn right across a footbridge and follow the path to a cottage, bearing right to a track. Turn left and head back to Bateman's. Retrace your steps to Burwash.

Brightling's Folly Trail

Step into the colourful world of 'Mad Jack' Fuller on this wonderfully varied exploration of the High Weald.

DISTANCE *5 miles (8km)* MINIMUM TIME *2hrs 30min*

ASCENT/GRADIENT *197ft (60m)* ▲▲▲ LEVEL OF DIFFICULTY +++

PATHS *Parkland paths, woodland bridleways and lanes, 1 stile*

LANDSCAPE *Parkland and dense woodland*

SUGGESTED MAP *OS Explorer 124 Hastings & Bexhill*

START / FINISH *Grid reference: TQ 683210*

DOG FRIENDLINESS *Off lead in woodland, but heed signs*

PARKING *Limited spaces by Brightling church. Avoid times of church services. Alternatively, park at Darwell Wood, south of Brightling, and begin at Point 4*

PUBLIC TOILETS *None on route*

To call John 'Mad Jack' Fuller an eccentric would be something of an understatement. His monuments and follies are scattered round the peaceful village of Brightling, where he lived. Long after Fuller's death in 1834, his name lives on, as does his reputation as a wilful, autocratic and larger-than-life character who embraced a wide range of interests and became a renowned patron of the arts.

Fuller's Fortune Secure

John Fuller was born in 1757, the son of a Hampshire rector. The family made its money from the Sussex iron industry, allowing the young John a privileged upbringing. He attended Eton and on his 20th birthday inherited the family fortune and its estates. His future was secure.

He came close to marriage in his 30s but his proposal was declined. Fuller remained a bachelor for the rest of his life, at first throwing himself headlong into politics. He stood for Parliament on several occasions and eventually became the Honourable Member for East Sussex. But Fuller was no ordinary MP. He was the stuff of which legends are made – swearing at the Speaker of the House of Commons, thundering down from London in a carriage with footmen armed to the teeth with pistols and drawn swords, refusing a peerage, consuming three bottles of port a day and engaging in reckless, impossible wagers.

'Mad Jack'

Hardly surprising he became known as 'Mad Jack'. With his 22-stone (140kg) frame and loud, bellowing voice, Fuller often induced fear in the strongest of souls. In fact, his quick temper and unpredictable nature eventually ruined his prospects of climbing the political ladder. After insulting the Speaker he was forcibly removed from the chamber by the Sergeant at Arms and told to apologise. He did not stand again for Parliament and quickly became disillusioned with politics. Instead, he focused his attention on folly-building.

BRIGHTLING

Explore Brightling and the surrounding countryside and you will see Fuller's follies everywhere, keeping alive his memory, reflecting his quirky nature and his taste for the absurd. Even his final resting place seems wildly over the top. This, his final folly, is a sandstone pyramid mausoleum erected in Brightling churchyard, where the walk begins. For many years people genuinely believed that Fuller had been interred in an upright position, dressed for dinner, holding a bottle of claret and wearing a top hat. When the tomb was eventually opened for restoration work, the rumours proved to be unfounded, though, given his exuberant personality, it would not be surprising if the gossip had been true.

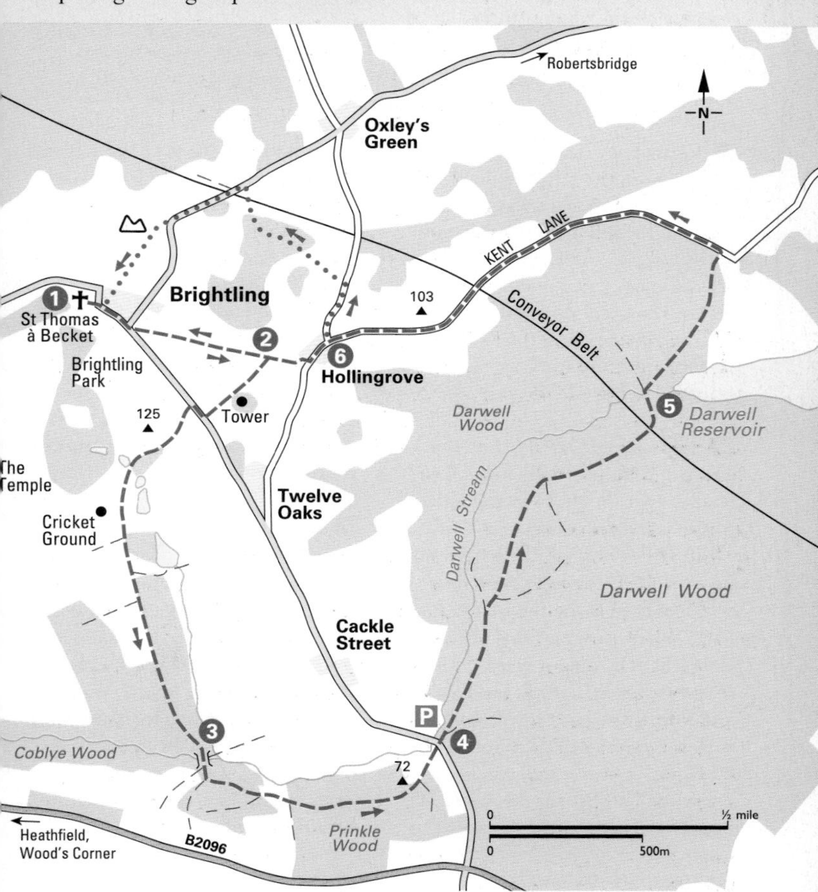

WALK 8 DIRECTIONS

❶ Enter the churchyard opposite Wealden House and walk through it, down to the road. Turn right, pass Brightling Park and make for a turning on the left, signposted 'Robertsbridge'. Go through a galvanised kissing gate by the junction and follow the clear path across the fields to a footpath junction and sign.

❷ Turn right here and follow the field-edge towards the Tower. Cross a stile on the right, cut through the trees and descend the field slope to the stile and

road. Bear right for a few paces, turning left by some barns and outbuildings. Cut between ponds and lakes and look for a cricket ground by the track. The Temple can be seen on the right at regular intervals along this stretch.
Pass a turning to some farm outbuildings and continue on the main bridleway, signed Coblye, keeping ahead when it forks.
Cut through an area of pheasant-rearing woodland and descend to a footbridge.

3 Cross the bridge, climb past a cottage on the left, then fork left and keep to the main track through Prinkle Wood, ignoring paths left and right. Eventually reach a gate, exit the wood and follow the track downhill to a gate and road. Cross into a wide parking area and look for two tracks into Darwell Wood.

4 Take the left-hand bridle track and when it eventually forks, keep to the right. Begin to swing left as the track curves around to the right, still following the bridleway. Keep right at the next waymark and continue along the forest path. When it swings sharply to the right at a hairpin bend, look for a bridleway sign on the left and follow the path through the wood. On emerging from the trees, cross over a pipe enclosing a conveyor belt linking Mountfield and Brightling gypsum mines.

WHAT TO LOOK OUT FOR

In the middle of Brightling Park, landscaped by 'Capability' Brown, stands the Grecian-style Rotunda Temple, a circular domed building. It may have been used as a hide-out for smugglers or a store for contraband. Alternatively, Fuller might have built it for gambling sessions or entertaining ladies. Darwell Reservoir is managed as a trout fishery and is popular with anglers and ornithologists.

5 Follow the track to the left and then veer right after a few steps at the fork. Cross over the Darwell Stream and bear right, following the woodland path up through the trees to the road. Turn right to glimpse Darwell Reservoir and turn left to continue the walk. Follow Kent Lane, recross the conveyor belt and make for the hamlet of Hollingrove. On the right here is an old chapel, which is now a house.

6 Keep left at the junction and walk along the lane for a short distance, passing Glebe Cottage. Take the stony track on the right and veer left after a few paces in front of a part tile-hung house (AEF 1840 on the front). Walk along to the turning for the Tower, visited near the start of the walk, then retrace your steps across the fields and follow the road back to Brightling church.

WHILE YOU'RE THERE

Have a look at the pyramid mausoleum and step inside the Parish Church of St Thomas à Becket. There's plenty to see and an audio guide enables you to pick out the various features. In addition to his love of architecture, John Fuller was a generous benefactor. His donations included the provision of a barrel organ in 1820. Near the start of the walk, close to the road, is one of Fuller's more accessible follies. The circular Tower, which dates back to the 1820s, is a two-storey, stone-built construction with a Gothic entrance and a top surrounded by battlements. Some sources suggest Fuller erected it so he could see Bodiam Castle, which he later bought for £3,000 to save it from demolition.

Around Brightling Woodlands

A longer version of Walk 8 takes in some fine mature woodland.

See map and information panel for Walk 8

DISTANCE *6 miles (9.7km)* MINIMUM TIME *3hrs*

ASCENT/GRADIENT *312ft (95m)* ▲▲▲ LEVEL OF DIFFICULTY +++

PATHS *Woodland, pasture and high ground, good views, 8 stiles*

WALK 9 DIRECTIONS (Walk 8 option)

To extend Walk 8 a little way further, turn right at Point 6, by the former chapel, and follow the lane north. Pass Hollytree Cottage and turn immediately left. After a few paces you reach a stile. Head diagonally right across the pasture, making for a curtain of woodland. Look for a stile in a gap in the trees and undergrowth, and go down the steps to a footbridge over a stream.

WHERE TO EAT AND DRINK

There are no refreshment facilities on either walk. When you finish your walk, try the Swan Inn at Wood's Corner, to the south-west of Brightling. A good range of food and drink is available and the pub has a cosy, welcoming atmosphere.

This is a very pleasant sheltered spot, the tree cover providing cooling shade on a warm day. Cross the bridge and bear right. The obvious, waymarked path cuts through the woodland, passing beneath overhanging holly trees. At a fork keep right, follow the waymarks and look for a stile on the far side of the wood. Pass between brambles to a further stile and then follow the path up some steps and over the gypsum mine conveyor belt, its low rumble often audible as you approach it.

After crossing the bridge, veer left to a stile as the track bends right. Cross the pasture to the next stile by a galvanised gate and exit to the road. Turn left and follow the road, passing a footpath on the right. Recross the conveyor belt and as the road begins to curve left, look for a stile and footpath sign on the right. Follow the path up the bank, through bracken, keeping parallel to the road. Head up the grassy hillside, go through a wide gateway and skirt the right edge of the field.

Glance back on this stretch to enjoy a truly superb view of rural Sussex. The trees of Darwell Wood cloak the landscape but somewhere deep within them lies the bridleway which forms the middle section of the main walk. Make for a stile ahead, partly concealed by holly trees. Turn left and follow the path to a gate and drive. Bear right and return to the centre of Brightling, emerging at the road by the church.

History and Science at Herstmonceux

A wooded walk passing a medieval castle and a 20th-century observatory.

DISTANCE *3 miles (4.8km)* MINIMUM TIME *1hr 30min*

ASCENT/GRADIENT *153ft (46m)* ▲▲▲ LEVEL OF DIFFICULTY +++

PATHS *Woodland and field paths, country lanes, 1 stile*

LANDSCAPE *Wood, farmland and parkland on edge of Pevensey Levels*

SUGGESTED MAP *OS Explorer 124 Hastings & Bexhill*

START / FINISH *Grid reference: TQ 654103*

DOG FRIENDLINESS *On a lead in woodland. Off lead on 1066 Country Walk*

PARKING *Small lay-by on Wartling Road, south of A271, near entrance to The Observatory Science Centre*

PUBLIC TOILETS *Castle and Science Centre, seasonal opening*

WALK 10 DIRECTIONS

Make for the entrance to the Science Centre, cross Wartling Road to a stile and enter the extensive woodland. Go over several tracks and continue on the straight footpath, picking your way through the trees. Eventually you reach a stile. Turn left, then immediately left into Wood Lane.

Follow the road alongside trees and cut between houses as you approach the road junction. Cross over to a bridleway sign set among the trees and go through a galvanised gate. Walk ahead along the concrete path as it threads its way through the woodland. Pass a reed-clogged lake and begin a gentle ascent between the trees. Keep ahead along the wide footpath, passing beneath the boughs of some fine beech trees and, when you emerge from the woodland, make for another galvanised gate.

Go through another gate on the left and then head across the field to reach a track. Keep left and veer left at a waymark after about 80yds (73m). Cross the field, heading up the slope to reach a line of trees. Look for a gate and follow the level path through the woodland. Cross over a path and then continue walking along the bridleway to the road.

Turn left and head for Herstmonceux church. Continue along the road to a gateway, joining forces now with the 1066 Country Walk. Bear left and follow the concrete drive to a gate by the entrance to Church Farmhouse. Cross over a tarmac lane serving the study centre and, as you descend the slope, the domes of the old observatory

WHERE TO EAT AND DRINK

The Lamb at nearby Wartling is an attractive 17th-century free house and restaurant. There is a tea room in the grounds of Herstmonceux Castle and plenty of picnic space at the Science Centre and Discovery Park.

WHAT TO LOOK OUT FOR

Herstmonceux church, which lies about 2 miles (3.2km) from the village centre, stands on a wooded rise, opposite one of the entrances to Herstmonceux Castle. The church, overlooking Pevensey Levels, is dedicated to All Saints, indicating it is probably of Saxon origin. As you join the 1066 Country Walk, you cannot fail to spot the white-domed satellite laser ranger, which belongs to the Royal Greenwich Observatory.

begin to peep into view above the trees, giving these rural surroundings an unexpectedly surreal, almost futuristic quality. Make for the next galvanised gate and here you get an impressive view of Herstmonceux Castle over on the left.

A romantic-looking 15th-century moated castle set in beautiful parkland and superb Elizabethan gardens, Herstmonceux perfectly captures the essence of medieval England. At the time William, Duke of Normandy, marched through Sussex to do battle with Harold and his Saxon army, Herstmonceux was probably no more than a small manor. *Herst* is a Saxon word meaning 'clearing' and Monceux comes from Drogo de Monceux, a relative of William. The land later passed to the Fiennes family, ancestors of Ralph Fiennes and his brother Joseph, two of Britain's leading modern film actors.

It was in 1441 that Sir Roger de Fiennes, treasurer of the royal household, applied for a royal licence to build a castle here, though he wanted to use it to entertain his friends, not to defend his country. Herstmonceux is perhaps the first example of a sham – a country pile disguised as a castle. Much of the interior was demolished in 1776 to build nearby Herstmonceux Place and, by Victorian times, it was little more than a romantic ruin.

The castle was rebuilt in 1911 and in 1947 it became the home of the Royal Greenwich Observatory. When the Observatory relocated again in 1987, due to increasing light pollution, the castle and grounds were bought by Queen's University, Ontario, for use as an international study centre.

In sharp contrast to the castle are the buildings of The Observatory Science Centre next door. These famous green domes originally housed six large equatorial telescopes belonging to the observatory. Between the 1950s and the 1980s, weather permitting, astronomers studied the stars and other night-sky phenomena here.

Cross a footpath to another gate. Begin a gradual, though not particularly steep, climb and continue on the 1066 Country Walk as it runs hard by the Science Centre boundary. Follow the woodland path to the road, turn left and return to the lay-by.

WHILE YOU'RE THERE

Visit the grounds of Herstmonceux Castle to see the walled garden (from before 1570), a herb garden, woodland sculptures and a folly. Walks take you to the remains of a 300-year-old sweet chestnut avenue, a rhododendron garden and a waterfall. The castle itself is not open to the public, but you can stop off at The Observatory Science Centre where astronomy exhibitions illustrate the work and history of the Observatory.

Romans and Normans at Pevensey

Visit a Norman castle within a Roman fort and experience the atmosphere of the eerie Pevensey Levels on this fascinating walk.

DISTANCE *4.5 miles (7.2km)* **MINIMUM TIME** *1hr 45min*

ASCENT/GRADIENT *Negligible* ▲▲▲ **LEVEL OF DIFFICULTY** +++

PATHS *Field paths, brief stretch of road and riverside, 4 stiles*

LANDSCAPE *Low-level former marshland, flat and watery landscape*

SUGGESTED MAP *OS Explorer 124 Hastings & Bexhill*

START / FINISH *Grid reference: TQ 645048*

DOG FRIENDLINESS *Under control on farmland and minor roads*

PARKING *Pay-and-display car park by Pevensey Castle*

PUBLIC TOILETS *At car park*

The great harbour here silted up long ago, leaving Pevensey stranded inland, 2 miles (3.2km) from the sea. It was from here that William, Duke of Normandy, marched inland to defeat King Harold and his Saxon army in 1066. What took place represents one of the most significant events in English history (See Walk 6).

Roman Fortress

The exact spot where William came ashore can never be identified, as the coastline has shifted and altered so greatly down the centuries. What is known, however, is that 800 years before the arrival of William, the Romans chose this site to construct the fortress of Anderida as part of their defence of the Saxon Shore. Pevensey was one of a series of fortifications along this coast and the remains of the outer walls of the castle survive. Standing up to 30ft (9m) thick in places and enclosing an oval area of about 10 acres (4ha), the walls are considered to be among the finest examples of Roman building in the world.

In 1066, centuries after the Roman invasion of Britain, William, Duke of Normandy, crossed the Channel and came ashore at Pevensey. Determined to claim the English crown, he expected to be met with some resistance at Anderida. But William found the fort undefended, enabling him to consolidate his position immediately. Harold and his men were elsewhere, fighting his brother's Danish army in Yorkshire and expecting William to sail via the Isle of Wight.

The Normans immediately set about erecting one of three prefabricated timber castles they had brought with them, constructing it on a mound of earth within the fort. It was as if they were intent on taking the place of the Romans who had occupied this site so many years before them. Without opposition, the Norman army travelled almost casually through the Sussex countryside, taking food from local people and burning and looting whatever they could find. Following the Battle of Hastings, William gave the stronghold to his half-brother, Robert, Count of Mortain. It was Robert who built the Norman castle, the remains of which we see today.

A keep and bailey were subsequently constructed and in the 13th century a formidable stone curtain wall and gatehouse were added.

Further Defences

Further work took place in the 14th century but by now the castle was sturdy enough to defend itself and its inhabitants from the strongest opponent. Pevensey was prepared to defend the coast from the threat of Napoleon and even as recently as 1940, pill boxes were installed into the castle walls should German forces invade.

This atmospheric walk starts at Pevensey Castle. After a brief tour of Pevensey, with its picturesque houses and cottages, head out across the lonely, evocative Pevensey Levels, once covered by water and now reminiscent of the fenland country of East Anglia.

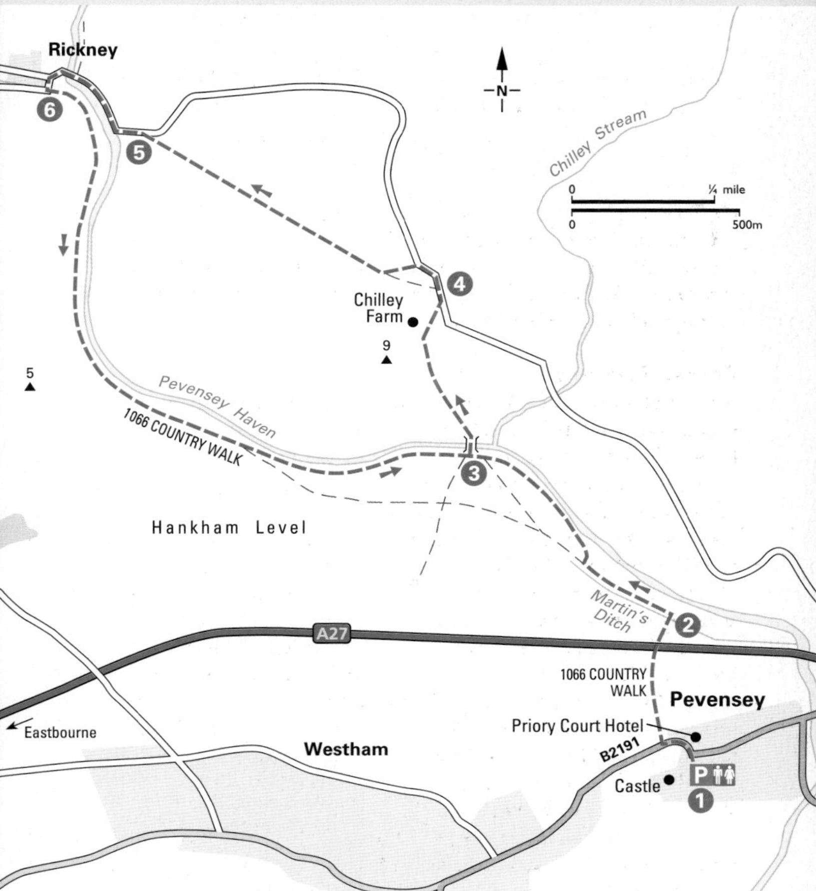

WALK 11 DIRECTIONS

1 On leaving the car park, go straight ahead on the bend and keep the Priory Court Hotel on the right. Pevensey Castle's walls rise up impressively on your left. Bear off to the right just beyond the hotel to follow the 1066 Country Walk.

❷ Cross the A27 and keep on the trail, following the sign for Rickney. Go through a gate and follow the path as it bends left. Continue between fencing and hedging; keep Martin's Ditch on the left and pass through a galvanised gate. Bear right to the river bank footpath sign and turn left alongside the Pevensey Haven, saunter past its confluence with the Chilley Stream.

WHERE TO EAT AND DRINK

Priory Court Hotel near the car park has a good selection of hot and cold food. Chilley Farm Shop serves tea, coffee and a range of tasty sandwiches and cakes. The Royal Oak and the Smugglers also serve food and the Castle Cottage tea room is very popular.

❸ Continue for a short distance to a footbridge. Cross over it and then aim half left, making for a house. Head for a footbridge in the line of bushes and then cross rough, thistle-strewn ground to two stiles in the corner by some trees. Bear diagonally right to a wooden gate, then turn right and walk along the track to the road passing Chilley Farm Shop.

❹ Swing left at the lane, follow it until it curves right and go through a gate on the left here. Follow the path to some gates and pass through the right-hand one. Keep ahead to a gate in the field corner and continue, keeping the boundary on your left. Make for a footbridge on the left. Cross it and bear right. Follow the edge of the pasture to reach two stiles and exit to the road.

❺ Keep left and walk along to the village of Rickney. Avoid the 1066 Country Walk as it runs off to the north and cross the little road bridge. Bear left at the sign for Hankham and immediately cross a bridge. Swing left after a few paces and follow the 1066 Country Walk.

WHILE YOU'RE THERE

Take a stroll through the ancient town of Pevensey and visit the fascinating Court House Museum in the High Street, once the smallest town hall in England. In 1882, under the Municipal Corporation Act, Pevensey lost its status as a borough and in 1890 the Pevensey Town Trust was established to administer the Court House. Inside, you can see the Court Room, Robing Room, cells and exercise yard. There are many exhibits and displays, including a silver penny of William I minted at Pevensey.

❻ Go through a gate, pass beside a barn to reach a galvanised gate and continue ahead along the right-hand field-edge, soon to reach the Pevensey Haven Walk beside the river. Pass the footbridge crossed earlier and then retrace your steps to the A27 and Pevensey.

WHAT TO LOOK OUT FOR

By the Pevensey Castle car park entrance is a plaque to commemorate a visit by Her Majesty Queen Elizabeth II on 28 October 1966 and the landing of William, Duke of Normandy on 28 September 1066.

A former coastal inlet which was drained mainly in the 14th and 15th centuries, the Pevensey Levels have their own individual character. This is a haven for wildlife, plants and insects, as well as home to a great variety of birds, both in summer and winter. Redshank, plovers, snipe and wildfowl visit in winter, while skylarks and kestrels are found here throughout the year.

Right: The walls of Pevensey Castle (Walk 11)

Birling Gap to Beachy Head

A magnificent clifftop walk exploring a scenic stretch of the Sussex coast.

DISTANCE *7 miles (11.2km)* MINIMUM TIME *3hrs*
ASCENT/GRADIENT *536ft (163m)* ▲▲▲ LEVEL OF DIFFICULTY +++
PATHS *Downland paths and tracks, clifftop greensward, no stiles*
LANDSCAPE *Southern boundary of South Downs and headland*
SUGGESTED MAP *OS Explorer 123 Eastbourne & Beachy Head*
START / FINISH *Grid reference:TQ 554959*
DOG FRIENDLINESS *On lead by Cornish Farm and on South Downs Way*
PARKING *Free car park at Birling Gap*
PUBLIC TOILETS *Birling Gap and Beachy Head*

The magnificent chalk cliffs of Beachy Head were formed from the shells of billions of minute creatures which fell to the bottom of a subtropical sea. Today, this stretch of coast is one of Britain's most famous landmarks. The treeless South Downs reach the sea in spectacular fashion and over 500ft (152m) below the towering cliffs lies Beachy Head's distinctive red and white lighthouse, standing alone on a remote beach. This blend of natural and artificial features creates a magnificent picture.

Devil's Cape

The present 142ft (43m) lighthouse, automated in 1983 and modernised in 1999, has been vital to the safety of mariners off this coast since it was completed in 1902. But even as far back as 1670 a beacon shone from this point, helping to guide ships away from the treacherous ledges below. Beachy Head has always been a navigational nightmare. Sailors have long feared it and the Venetians dubbed it the Devil's Cape. In 1831 the eccentric Sussex landowner John Fuller (See Walk 8), or 'Mad Jack' as he was known, built the Belle Tout lighthouse high up on the headland to the west of Beachy Head. The lamp was first lit in 1834 but the lighthouse was never a great success. Its lofty position on the cliff top meant that it was often shrouded in mist and fog and therefore invisible to shipping in the English Channel. A decision was eventually taken to erect a lighthouse at sea level.

Everyone has heard of Beachy Head but not many of us know where the name originates. It comes from the Norman French *Beau Chef* – meaning beautiful headland. The description is certainly apt and this breezy, sprawling cliff top draws visitors and tourists from far and wide who come to marvel at the breathtaking sea views or saunter along the South Downs Way. The whole area is a designated Site of Special Scientific Interest (SSSI).

The walk begins at Birling Gap to the west of Beachy Head. Before long it heads inland, running across the slopes of the South Downs. Within sight of Eastbourne, it suddenly switches direction, following the South Downs Way to Beachy Head and back to Birling Gap. On the way it passes the old Belle Tout lighthouse, now a private home.

Left: The Seven Sisters from Beachy Head (Walk 12)

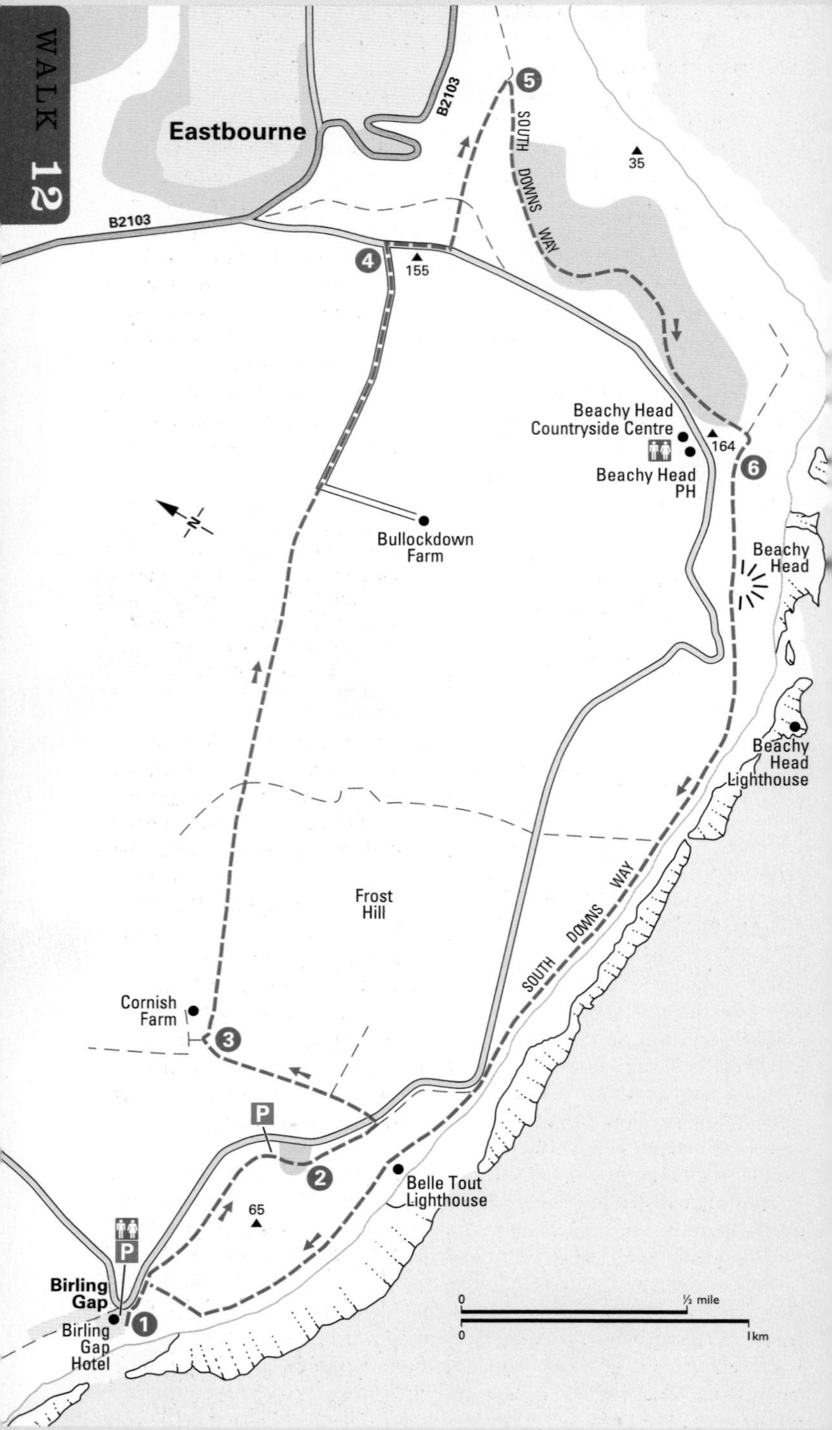

Eastbourne
B2103
B2103
5
SOUTH DOWNS WAY
35
4
155
Beachy Head Countryside Centre
164
6
Beachy Head PH
Bullockdown Farm
N
Beachy Head
Beachy Head Lighthouse
SOUTH DOWNS WAY
Frost Hill
Cornish Farm
3
P
2
Belle Tout Lighthouse
65
P
Birling Gap
1
Birling Gap Hotel
0 ½ mile
0 1km

WALK 12 DIRECTIONS

1 Walk away from the car park, keeping the road on your left. Ignore the South Downs Way sign by the road and continue on the grassy path. Keep to the right of the next car park and follow the path between the trees.

2 Keep parallel to the road and when you see a junction with a concrete track, take the next left path down to meet it. Follow the bridleway signposted 'East Dean Down'. Glance back here for an unexpected view of the old Belle Tout lighthouse. Pass a fingerpost and continue ahead.

3 Follow the concrete track as it bends right towards Cornish Farm, avoiding the bridleway going straight on. Look for a gate on the right and head east, keeping the fence on your right-hand side. Make for another gate and continue ahead. Pass alongside lines of bushes before reaching the next gate. Traffic on the A259 zips by on the skyline. Pass an access track to Bullockdown Farm and along here you can see flint walls enclosing fields and pastures.

WHILE YOU'RE THERE

Beachy Head Countryside Centre is both educational and entertaining. The centre illustrates the history of the area and its coastline. There are innovative interactive displays on shepherding and Bronze Age life, touch-screen computers and hands-on wildlife displays.

4 Pass beside a barrier to the road and turn right, following the wide grassy verge. On reaching two adjoining gates on the right, cross the road and take the grassy path down to a waymarked junction. Follow the path towards Eastbourne, signposted 'seafront'; soon meet the South Downs Way.

5 Bear sharp right here and follow the long distance trail as it climbs steadily between bushes and vegetation. Keep right when another path comes in from the left and make for a viewpoint, with the first glimpse of Beachy Head lighthouse at the foot of the cliff. Cross the grass, up the slope to the trig point. In front of you now are the Beachy Head pub and Beachy Head Countryside Centre.

WHERE TO EAT AND DRINK

The Birling Gap Hotel has a bar, carvery and coffee shop. The Beachy Head pub has a bar, restaurant and coffee shop. It gets very busy on summer days and bank holidays.

6 Return to the South Downs Way and follow it west. The path can be seen ahead, running over the undulating cliff top. Keep the Belle Tout lighthouse in your sights and follow the path up towards it. Keep to the right of the old lighthouse and soon the car park at Birling Gap edges into view, as do the famous Seven Sisters cliffs. Bear right at the South Downs Way post and follow the path down and round to the left. Swing left just before the road and return to the car park.

WHAT TO LOOK OUT FOR

Up on the cliff, above Beachy Head lighthouse, lies the site of a 19th-century signalling station. Messages were sent from here to the London offices of Lloyd's confirming the safe arrival of ships and their cargoes. The station closed in 1904.

The Snake River and the Seven Sisters

Follow a breezy trail beside the Cuckmere River as it winds in erratic fashion towards the sea.

DISTANCE *3 miles (4.8km)* MINIMUM TIME *1hr 30min*

ASCENT/GRADIENT *Negligible* ▲▲▲ LEVEL OF DIFFICULTY +++

PATHS *Grassy trails and well-used paths, mostly beside the Cuckmere or canalised branch of river*

LANDSCAPE *Exposed and isolated valley and river mouth*

SUGGESTED MAP *OS Explorer 123 Eastbourne & Beachy Head*

START / FINISH *Grid reference: TV 518995*

DOG FRIENDLINESS *Under close control within Seven Sisters Country Park. On lead during lambing season and near A259*

PARKING *Fee-paying car park at Seven Sisters Country Park*

PUBLIC TOILETS *Opposite car park, by visitor centre*

One of the few remaining undeveloped river mouths in the south-east, is the gap or cove known as Cuckmere Haven. It is one of the south coast's best-known and most popular beauty spots and was regularly used by smugglers in the 18th century to bring ashore their cargoes of brandy and lace. The scene has changed very little in the intervening years with the eternal surge of waves breaking on the isolated shore.

The Cuckmere River joins the English Channel at this point, but not before it makes a series of extraordinarily wide loops through lush water-meadows. It's hardly surprising that this characteristic has earned it the occasional epithet 'Snake River'. Winding ever closer to the sea, the Cuckmere emerges beside the famous white chalk cliffs known as the Seven Sisters. Extending east towards Birling Gap, there are, in fact, eight of these towering chalk faces, with the highest one, Haven Brow (253ft/77m), closest to the river mouth. On the other side of the estuary rise the cliffs of Seaford Head, a nature reserve run by the local authority.

Seven Sisters Country Park

The focal point of the lower valley is the Seven Sisters Country Park, an amenity area of 692 acres (280ha) developed by East Sussex County Council. The site is a perfect location for a country park and has been imaginatively planned to blend with the coastal beauty of this fascinating area. There are artificial lakes and park trails, and an old Sussex barn near by has been converted to provide a visitor centre which includes many interesting exhibits and displays.

However, there is more to the park than just these attractions. Wildlife plays a key role within the park's boundaries, providing naturalists with hours of pleasure and enjoyment. The flowers and insects found here are at their best in early to mid summer, while spring and autumn are a good time to bring your binoculars with you for a close-up view of migrant birds.

A Haven for Birds

Early migrant wheatears are sometimes spotted in the vicinity of the river mouth from late February onwards and are followed later in the season by martins, swallows, whinchats and warblers. Keep a careful eye out for whitethroats, terns and waders too. The lakes and lagoons tend to attract waders such as curlews, sandpipers and little stints. Grey phalaropes have also been seen in the park, usually after severe autumn storms. These elusive birds spend most of their lives far out to sea, usually off South America or western Africa.

The walk explores this very special part of the Cuckmere Valley and begins by heading for the beach. As you make your way there, you might wonder why the river meanders the way it does. The meltwaters of the last Ice Age shaped this landscape, and over the centuries rising sea levels and a freshwater peat swamp influenced the river's route to the Channel. Around the start of the 19th century, the sea rose to today's level and a new straight cut with raised banks, devised in 1846, shortened the Cuckmere's journey to the sea. This unnatural waterway controls the river and helps prevent flooding in the valley.

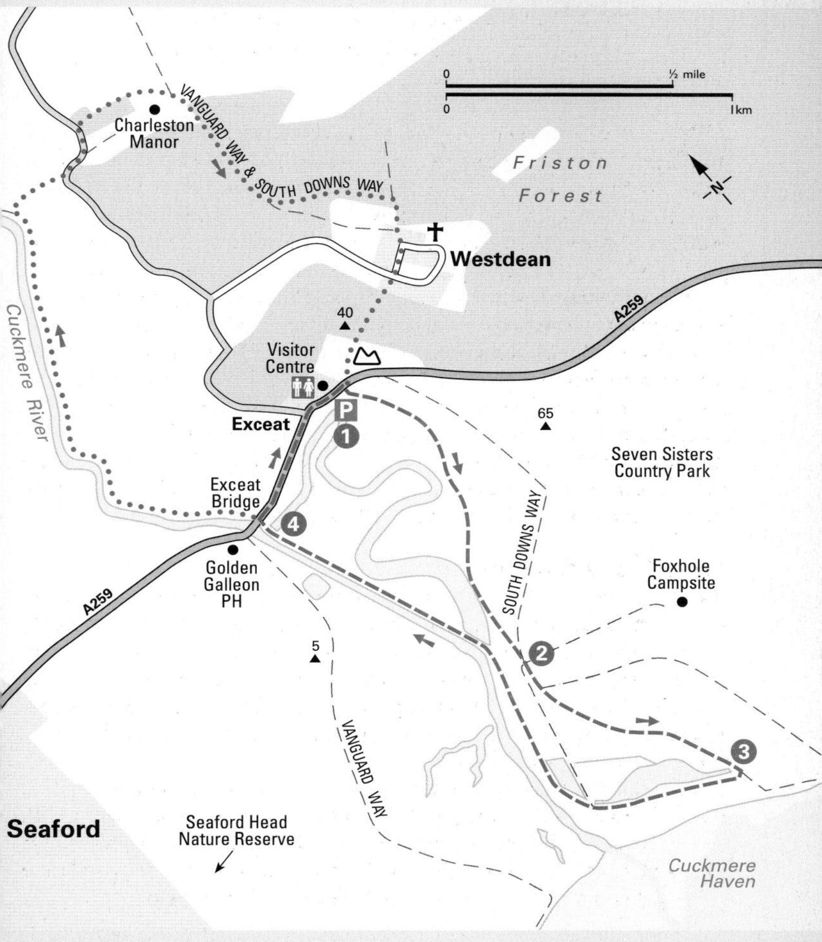

WALK 13 DIRECTIONS

1 Make for the gate situated near the entrance to the Seven Sisters Country Park and follow the wide, grassy path towards the beach. The path gradually curves to the right, running alongside a concrete track. The Cuckmere River meanders beside you, heading for the open sea. Continue ahead between the track and the river and make for a South Downs Way sign.

WHERE TO EAT AND DRINK

The Golden Galleon by Exceat Bridge is a very popular 18th-century inn thought to have inspired Rudyard Kipling's poem *Song of the Smugglers*. The menu is traditional and very British, with various other dishes. The visitor centre at the Seven Sisters Country Park has a restaurant and tea rooms and in summer there is often an ice cream van in the car park.

2 Avoid the long distance trail as it runs in from the left, pass it and the Foxhole campsite and keep ahead, through the gate towards the beach. Veer left at the beach and South Downs Way sign. On reaching the next gate, don't go through it. Instead, keep right and follow the beach sign. Pass a couple of wartime pill boxes on the left, an evocative reminder of less peaceful times, and go through a gate. Join a stony path and walk ahead to the beach, with the white wall of the Seven Sisters rearing up beside you.

WHAT TO LOOK OUT FOR

Shingle plants thrive on the sheltered parts of beaches and a stroll at Cuckmere Haven reveals the yellow horned-poppy and the fleshy leaved sea kale. Sea beet, curled dock and scentless chamomile also grow here.

3 Turn right and cross the shore, approaching a Cuckmere Haven Emergency Point sign. Branch off to the right to join another track here. Follow this for about 50yds (46m) until you come to a junction and keep left, following the Park Trail. Keep beside the Cuckmere and the landscape here is characterised by a network of meandering channels and waterways, all feeding into the river. Pass a turning for Foxhole campsite and follow the footpath as it veers left, in line with the Cuckmere. Make for a kissing gate and continue on the straight path by the side of the river.

4 Keep ahead to the road at Exceat Bridge and on the left is the Golden Galleon pub. Turn right and follow the A259 to return to the car park at the country park.

WHILE YOU'RE THERE

If you have the time, take a look at the Seaford Head Nature Reserve, which lies on the west side of Cuckmere Haven. This chalk headland, which rises 282ft (85m) above the sea, is a popular local attraction and from here the coastal views are magnificent.

Cuckmere River and Charleston Manor

A longer walk up the Cuckmere Valley to a 12th-century manor house and the quiet village of Westdean.

See map and information panel for Walk 13

DISTANCE *5.5 miles (8.8km)* MINIMUM TIME *3hrs*

ASCENT/GRADIENT *262ft (80m)* ▲▲▲ LEVEL OF DIFFICULTY +++

PATHS *Valley and thick woodland, 6 stiles*

DOG FRIENDLINESS *Several stretches of road. Under control in Friston Forest*

WALK 14 DIRECTIONS (Walk 13 option)

To make a longer walk in the Cuckmere Valley, cross Exceat Bridge at Point 4 and continue beside the Cuckmere, following the riverside path through this delightful, though lonely, valley. Swans may be seen gliding on the water. Head for a kissing gate, continue over several stiles and look for a path on the right, just before a stile.

Take the path away from the Cuckmere, following it between trees and bushes. Cross a stile, turn left at the road and pass the entrance to Charleston Manor. Pevsner described Charleston as 'a perfect house in a perfect setting.' Parts of it date from the early 12th century and the house is renowned for its truly splendid gardens and 15th-century double tithe barn.

Continue for a few paces and turn right to join a path signposted 'Jevington'. Merge with the South Downs Way and the Vanguard Way and keep right at the fork. Climb the steps and follow the pretty path first south, then south-east through Friston Forest. Veer left at the fork and cut through beech woodland to a clear junction.

Turn right here and make for the picturesque hamlet of Westdean, lying half-hidden in a wooded hollow. The church dates mostly from the 14th century and the old rectory beside it is probably Norman. Join the road on a bend and continue ahead to a junction. Cross over and walk ahead to a flight of steps.

Make for a stone stile at the top of the steps, where there are glorious views of the Cuckmere River below winding away towards the sea. This certainly has to be one of the most dramatic and memorable views in all of Sussex. Descend the steep, grassy hillside and make for a kissing gate by the visitor centre. Cross the road and return to the car park.

WALK 15

Lasting Impressions at Berwick

Beginning in the Cuckmere Valley, this breezy walk climbs high on to the Downs before visiting a church renowned for its wall painting.

DISTANCE *4 miles (6.4km)* MINIMUM TIME *2hrs*

ASCENT/GRADIENT *464ft (141m)* ▲▲▲ LEVEL OF DIFFICULTY +++

PATHS *Exposed paths and tracks, 1 stile*

LANDSCAPE *Downland to west of Cuckmere Valley*

SUGGESTED MAP *OS Explorer 123 Eastbourne & Beachy Head*

START / FINISH *Grid reference: TQ 520033*

DOG FRIENDLINESS *Mostly off lead but not permitted at Alfriston Clergy House*

PARKING *The Willows fee-paying car park, Alfriston*

PUBLIC TOILETS *Alfriston*

WALK 15 DIRECTIONS

With its charming shops, inns and parish church, Alfriston is a classic Sussex village and a key attraction on the tourist trail – posters showing the village fair were used to inspire British troops during the Second World War. Situated at the foot of the South Downs in a gap fashioned by the Cuckmere River, it's the perfect place to explore on foot. The church, known as the 'Cathedral of the Downs', occupies a secluded setting by a spacious green, hidden away from the main street. Standing on an ancient Anglo-Saxon mound, it is said to mark the spot where four oxen, carrying building materials, lay down to rest.

WHILE YOU'RE THERE

Visit the National Trust's Clergy House at Alfriston. This oak-framed, thatched building dates back to about 1350 and was built to cater for a number of confined parish priests in the aftermath of the Black Death. The National Trust acquired the Clergy House as their very first property in 1896, paying just £10 for it!

Turn left on leaving the car park and make for the centre of Alfriston. Pass the cross in the main street and turn right by the Star inn, following Star Lane. Go straight over at the junction King's Ride and continue on the South Downs Way. The road dwindles into a steep flinty track further up. This was originally a drovers' route for sheep being driven to market. Pass a bridleway on the right and follow the wide track as it curves gently to the right.

This stretch of the walk is dominated by glorious views over the Downs and towards Alfriston. As the track begins to veer left, keep right and continue on the South Downs Way. Go straight over a junction and keep going over this high ground until you see a gate on the right.

Turn right here for Berwick, following the path between

WHAT TO LOOK OUT FOR

On the edge of the green at Alfriston is an old mine, washed up on the Cuckmere River in October 1943 and rendered inactive by the naval authorities in the Second World War. Read the notice which invites you to spare a coin – 'in grateful thanks that Alfriston is not just another ruin which would have been the case had the mine exploded'.

fences. Descend to the left by clumps of gorse bushes and look for Berwick church in the distance. The smooth expanse of Arlington Reservoir is also visible. Go through a gate and 75yds (68m) beyond it turn sharp right at a junction.

Follow the clear path across the fields, keeping right at a fork. The path runs along the foot of the grassy slopes, cutting between trees and bushes. Bear right to join a track, then immediately swing left. Pass a bridleway on the right and continue on the track. Swing right when you see a sign for farm vehicles and walk along to the Cricketers Arms.

Join the path opposite the pub and follow the Vanguard Way. Keep right by the pond, pass beside a house and head for a stile. Cross a field towards the shingled broach spire of Berwick church, heading for a stile to the left of it. Enter the churchyard and visit 14th-century St Michaels and All Angels.

Inside look for the time switch and light up the interior of the church. That way you can appreciate the magnificent wall paintings in all their glory. These brilliant murals were commissioned by Bishop Bell of Chichester in 1943 and are the work of Duncan Grant and Vanessa and Quentin Bell, members of the renowned Bloomsbury Group.

During the Second World War many church windows were destroyed by bombs and the Bishop of Chichester considered it more appropriate for artists to decorate church walls rather than design windows. Familiar landmarks were used in the paintings and local people took part as models. In one scene, over the chancel arch, a soldier and airman from Firle and a sailor from Berwick are seen kneeling.

Leave by the same route, returning to the Vanguard Way. Go straight on at the right-hand bend, heading towards Alfriston. Descend to a gate and follow the waymarked path across open fields, then climb to join a gravel drive. Go straight ahead at the junction, avoiding Winton Street on the left. Descend the slope into Alfriston, bear left for the car park or continue ahead into the village.

WHERE TO EAT AND DRINK

The Star at Alfriston describes itself as the hotel that likes to say 'yes' to locals and visitors. There are log fires in winter, and breakfast, morning coffee and bar meals are served throughout the year. The timbered 14th-century George in the High Street is a cosy place to stop. Oak beams and a large inglenook fireplace add to the charm and fresh local fish appears on the menu. The Singing Kettle and Badgers Tea House both serve morning coffee, light lunches and afternoon tea and are located in the village centre. The Cricketers Arms at Berwick serves traditional home-made food, with the emphasis on local produce, meat and fish.

Wilmington's Mystery of the Long Man

This magnificent downland walk visits a legendary chalk figure which has baffled archaeologists and historians for hundreds of years.

DISTANCE *6.25 miles (10km)* MINIMUM TIME *2hrs 30min*

ASCENT/GRADIENT *465ft (152m)* ▲▲▲ LEVEL OF DIFFICULTY +++

PATHS *Downland paths and tracks, stretch of country road, 1 stile*

LANDSCAPE *Dramatic downland on east side of Cuckmere Valley*

SUGGESTED MAP *OS Explorer 123 Eastbourne & Beachy Head*

START / FINISH *Grid reference: TQ 543042*

DOG FRIENDLINESS *Some enclosed tracks suitable for dogs off lead*

PARKING *Free long-stay car park at Wilmington*

PUBLIC TOILETS *At car park*

One of Britain's most impressive and enduring mysteries is the focal point of this glorious walk high on the Downs. Cut into the turf below Windover Hill, the chalk figure of the Long Man of Wilmington is the largest representation of the human figure in western Europe and yet it remains an enigma, its origins shrouded in mystery. For centuries experts have been trying to solve this ancient puzzle but no one has been able to prove conclusively who he is or what he symbolises.

Helmeted War-god

For many years the earliest record of the Long Man was thought to have been a drawing by the antiquarian William Burrell, made when he visited Wilmington Priory in 1766. Then, in 1993, a new drawing was discovered, made by John Rowley, a surveyor, as long ago as 1710.

Though the new drawing has confirmed some theories, it has not been able to shed any real light as to the Long Man's true identity or why this particular hillside was chosen. However, it does suggest that the original figure was a shadow or indentation in the grass rather than a bold line. It seems there were distinguishing facial features which may have long faded; the staves being held were not a rake and a scythe as once described and the head was originally a helmet shape, indicating that the Long Man may have been a helmeted war-god.

Until the 19th century the chalk figure was only visible in a certain light, particularly when there was a dusting of snow or frost on the ground. In 1874, a public subscription was raised through *The Times* and the figure re-cut. To help define the outline of the Long Man, the site was marked out in yellow bricks, though this restoration work may have resulted in the feet being incorrectly positioned.

Camouflaged

In 1925 the Long Man of Wilmington was given to the Sussex Archaeological Trust, which later became the Sussex Archaeological Society, and during the Second World War the site was camouflaged to prevent enemy aircraft from using it as a landmark. In 1969 further restoration work began and the yellow bricks were replaced with pre-cast concrete blocks. These are frequently painted now, so that the shape of the Long Man stands out from a considerable distance away.

Photographed from the air, the figure is elongated, but when viewed from ground level an optical illusion is created and he assumes normal human proportions. The walk passes as close as it can to the Long Man before heading out into isolated downland country where the trees of Friston can be seen cloaking the landscape. Do this walk on a cold winter's day and the Long Man's ghostly aura, and the remoteness of the surroundings, will be enough to send a shiver down the spine.

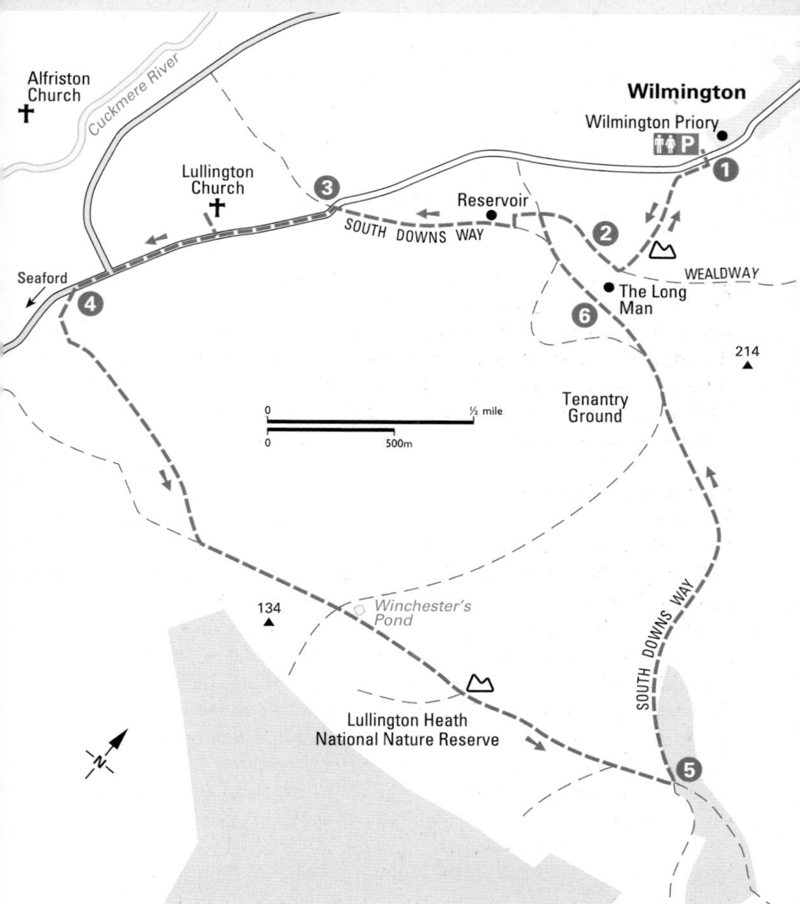

WALK 16 DIRECTIONS

1 Make for the car park exit and follow the path parallel to the road, heading towards the Long Man of Wilmington. Bear left at the stile and take the Wealdway to the chalk figure. Climb quite steeply, curving to the right. Go through a gate, avoid the Wealdway arrow and go straight ahead towards the escarpment, veering right just below the figure of the Long Man.

❷ Go through the next gate, cross a track and bear left on reaching a fence. A few paces brings you to a gate and a sign for the South Downs Way. Turn right, pass a small reservoir and follow the track to the road.

❸ Turn left and walk down to a signpost for Lullington church, following the path alongside several cottages. After visiting the church, retrace your steps to the road and turn right. Head down the lane and look for Alfriston church on the right. Pass a turning to the village on the right and continue ahead towards Seaford. Look out for a post box and swing left here, signposted 'Jevington'.

WHERE TO EAT AND DRINK

At the far end of the car park is a pleasant picnic area. The Giant's Rest in Wilmington is a popular pub at the northern end of the village. Alternatively, by the A27 is the Wishing Well Tea Rooms serving home-made soups, sandwiches and cakes.

❹ Follow the bridleway as it climbs steadily between tracts of remote downland. Keep left at the next main junction and there is a moderate climb. Avoid the bridle track branching off to the left and continue ahead towards Jevington. Lullington Heath National Nature Reserve is on the right now. Pass a bridleway on the right and keep on the track as it climbs steeply. Pass a second sign and also a map for the nature reserve and make for a junction with the South Downs Way.

WHILE YOU'RE THERE

Make a detour to look at the Lullington Heath National Nature Reserve, which consists of scrubland, chalk grassland and the best example of chalk heath still surviving in Britain. Various heathers and orchids also grow here. Study the maps displayed along the reserve boundary to help you follow the reserve's paths and bridleways.

❺ Turn left and follow the enclosed path to a gate. Go straight ahead alongside woodland and pass through a second gate. The path begins a gradual curve to the left and eventually passes along the rim of a spectacular dry valley known as Tenantry Ground. Keep the fence on your left and look for a gate ahead. Swing right as you approach it to a stile and then follow the path alongside the fence, crossing along the top of the Long Man.

❻ Glance to your right and you can just make out the head and body of the chalk figure down below. It's an intriguing view. Continue keeping the fence on the right and descend to a gate. Turn right here and retrace your steps to the car park at Wilmington.

WHAT TO LOOK OUT FOR

Wilmington Priory was founded for the Benedictine abbey of Grestain in Normandy, and much of the present building dates from the 14th century. As few as two or three monks resided here and they used the parish church in Wilmington rather than build their own place of worship. The monks were engaged in managing the abbey's English estates. The priory is in the care of the Landmark Trust and used as a holiday let, so not open to the public. Only 16ft (5m) square, 13th-century Lullington church stands above the Cuckmere valley and is one of Britain's smallest churches.

Arlington's Lakeside Trail

Combine this delightful walk with a little birding as you explore the banks of a reservoir by the Cuckmere River.

DISTANCE *3 miles (4.8km)* **MINIMUM TIME** *1hr 30min*

ASCENT/GRADIENT *82ft (25m)* ▲▲▲ **LEVEL OF DIFFICULTY** +++

PATHS *Field paths and trail, some brief road walking, 13 stiles*

LANDSCAPE *Level lakeside terrain and gentle farmland*

SUGGESTED MAP *OS Explorer 123 Eastbourne & Beachy Head*

START / FINISH *Grid reference: TQ 528074*

DOG FRIENDLINESS *Mostly on lead, as requested by signs en route*

PARKING *Fee-paying car park at Arlington Reservoir*

PUBLIC TOILETS *At car park*

It was in 1971 that Arlington's rural landscape changed irrevocably in both character and identity. A vital new reservoir was opened, supplying water to the nearby communities of Eastbourne, Hailsham, Polegate and Heathfield. Study the informative blurb on the grassy bank and you'll learn that the area of the reservoir is equivalent to 121 football pitches and that the maximum depth of the lake is 37ft (11.3m), deep enough to submerge four single-decker buses.

Fishing

The 120-acre (46ha) reservoir was formed by cleverly cutting off a meander in the Cuckmere River and it's now an established site for wintering wildfowl, as well as home to a successful rainbow trout fishery. Besides the trout, bream, perch, roach and eels make up Arlington's underwater population. Fly fishing is a popular activity here and the lake draws anglers from all over Sussex.

The local nature reserve was originally planted with more than 30,000 native trees, including oak, birch, wild cherry, hazel and hawthorn. The grassland areas along the shoreline are intentionally left uncut to enable many kinds of moth and butterfly to thrive in their natural habitats. Orchids grow here too.

Bird Watching

Arlington Reservoir, a designated Site of Special Scientific Interest (SSSI), is a favourite haunt of many birds on spring and autumn migrations and up to 10,000 wildfowl spend their winter here, including large numbers of mallard and wigeon. The shoveler duck is also a frequent visitor and most common as a bird of passage. You can identify the head of the shoveler drake by its dark, bottle-green colouring and broad bill. The breast is white and the underparts bright chestnut, while its brown and black back has a noticeable blue sheen. The female duck is mottled brown.

Great crested grebes, Canada geese and nightingales are also known to inhabit the reservoir area, making Arlington a popular destination for ornithologists. See if you can spot the blue flash of a kingfisher on the water, its colouring so distinctive it would be hard to confuse it with any other bird. It's also known for its piercing whistles as it swoops low over the water. The reservoir and its environs are also home to fallow deer and foxes, so keep a sharp look-out as you walk around the lake.

The walk begins in the main car park by the reservoir, though initially views of the lake are obscured by undergrowth and a curtain of trees. Be patient. After visiting the village of Arlington, where there is a welcome pub, the return leg is directly beside the water, providing a constantly changing scenic backdrop to round off the walk.

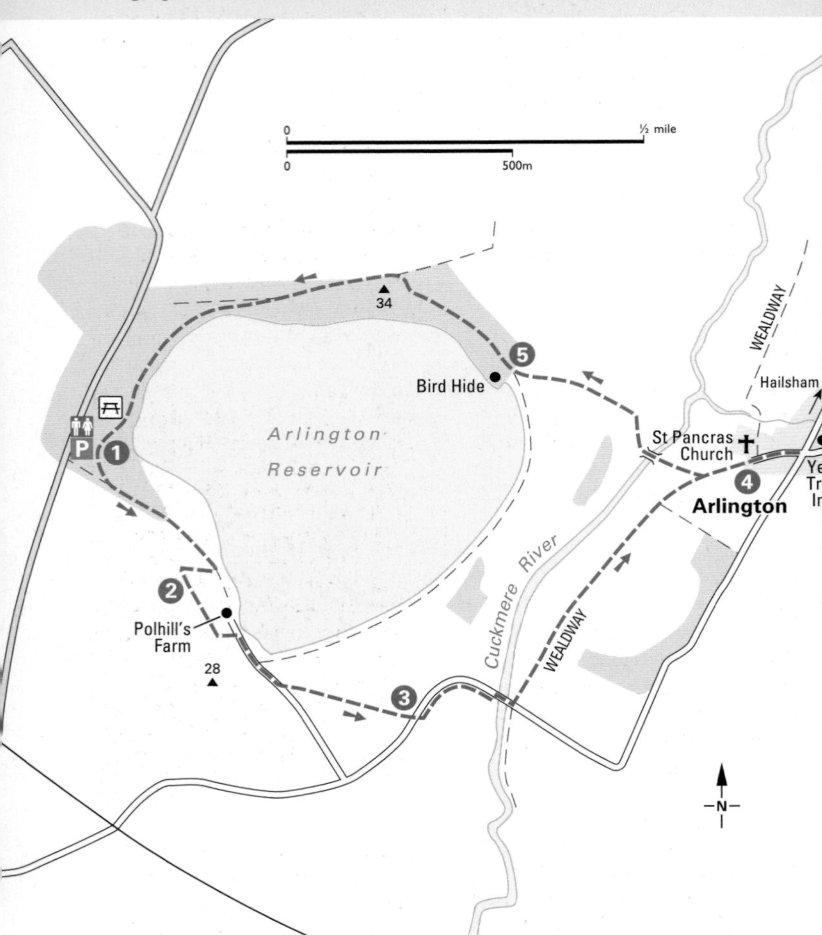

WALK 17 DIRECTIONS

❶ From the car park walk towards the information boards and then turn right to join the waymarked bridleway. Cut through the trees to a tarmac lane and look for a bridleway sign. Follow the lane and soon the reservoir edges into view again. On reaching a gate signed 'No entry – farm access only' bear right and follow the bridleway and footpath signs.

WHERE TO EAT AND DRINK

Arlington Reservoir has a picnic site by the car park where you can relax before or after the walk. The Yew Tree Inn at Arlington has a children's play area, beer garden and a choice of home-cooked dishes. Lunch and dinner are served every day and there is a choice of real ales. Nearby is the Old Oak Inn, originally the village almshouse and dating from 1733. The likes of Newhaven cod in batter, curry and steak-and-kidney pudding feature on the menu.

2 Skirt the buildings of Polhill's Farm and return to walk along the tarmac lane. Turn right and walk along to a kissing gate and a 'circular walk' sign. Ignore the gate and keep on the lane. Continue for about 100yds (91m) and then branch left over a stile into a field. Swing half right and look for a second stile to the right of an overgrown pond. Cross a third stile and go across a pasture to a fourth stile.

3 Cross the road and follow the path parallel with the road. Rejoin the road, cross the Cuckmere River and then bear left to join the Wealdway, following the sign for Arlington. Walk along the drive and when it curves to the right, by some houses, veer left over a stile. The spire of Arlington church can be seen now. Continue ahead when you reach the right-hand fence corner, following the waymark. Cross several stiles and a footbridge. Keep to the right of the church, cross another stile and pass the Old School on the right.

WHAT TO LOOK OUT FOR

Call into Arlington's St Pancras Church. One of the most interesting churches in Sussex, it's built of flint and the nave dates back to Saxon times. Look closely and you can see that there are many examples of different architectural styles. Buy a copy of the guide to the church to enable you to learn more details about this fascinating place of worship.

4 Walk along the lane to the Yew Tree Inn, then retrace your steps to the church and cross over the field to the footbridge. Turn right immediately beyond it to a stile in the field corner. Cross the pasture to the obvious footbridge and continue to cross over a plank bridge, then head across the field towards a line of trees, following the vague outline of a path. The reservoir's embankment is clearly defined on the left, as you begin a gentle ascent.

WHILE YOU'RE THERE

Stop off at the Arlington bird hide, opened in 1996, and see if you can identify members of Arlington's feathered population. In spring you might spot an osprey, a large bird which occasionally visits lakes, fens and estuaries and preys almost exclusively on fish. Look out too for house martins, sand martins, sandpipers, blackcaps, kestrels, mallards and dunlins – among other birds. If you are interested in ornithology, a visit to the bird hide is a must.

5 Cross a stile by a galvanised gate and go through a kissing gate on the immediate right. Follow the path alongside the lake and pass a bird hide on the left. Turn left further on and keep to the bridleway as it reveals glimpses of the lake through the trees. Veer left at the fork and then follow the path alongside the reservoir back to the car park.

Fine Downland Views Over Feudal Firle

Climb high above a sprawling estate and look towards distant horizons on this superb downland walk.

DISTANCE *4.25 miles (6.8km)* **MINIMUM TIME** *2hrs*
ASCENT/GRADIENT *476ft (145m)* ▲▲▲ **LEVEL OF DIFFICULTY** +++
PATHS *Tracks, paths and roads*
LANDSCAPE *Downland and farmland*
SUGGESTED MAP *OS Explorer 123 Eastbourne & Beachy Head*
START / FINISH *Grid reference: TQ 468075*
DOG FRIENDLINESS *On lead in vicinity of Firle Place and near livestock*
PARKING *Free car park in Firle*
PUBLIC TOILETS *Firle Place and Charleston Farmhouse*

Stroll along the South Downs Way between Alfriston and the River Ouse and you can look down towards the sleepy village of Firle, nestling amid a patchwork of fields and hedgerows below the escarpment. There is something that sets this place apart from most other communities. Firle is an estate village with a tangible feudal atmosphere.

Firle Place: a Palladian Mansion

At the centre of the village lies Firle Place, home to the Gage family for over 500 years and now open to the public. The 18th-century house is magnificent, though it hardly looks classically English. It's built of a pale stone specially imported from Caen in Normandy, with hipped roof, dormers and a splendid Venetian window surmounting the rusticated central archway in the east front.

Firle Place is surrounded by glorious parkland and set against a magnificent backdrop of hanging woods. The name is Old English and means 'oak'. No house could occupy a finer location. A tour of the house reveals some fascinating treasures, many of which were brought back from America by Sir Thomas. The paintings include an important collection of Old Masters with works by Van Dyck, Reynolds, Gainsborough and Rubens, and there are also collections of Sèvres porcelain and English and French furniture.

A Place in History

The present Palladian mansion conceals part of an older Tudor building. This was later enlarged by Sir John Gage, Vice Chamberlain and Captain of the Royal Guard in the court of Henry VIII. In 1542, when James V of Scotland was killed at Solway Moss, he commanded the King's troops against the Scottish army. He also superintended the executions of Queen Catherine Howard and Lady Jane Grey, while Constable of the Tower of London. Sir Edward, his son, as Sheriff of Sussex, was responsible for ensuring that the Lewes Martyrs were burned, but the family later converted to the Roman Catholic faith and were forced to retire from public life.

Little remains of the external features of the original courtyard house. The house underwent major changes in 1745, remodelled by General Sir Thomas Gage who was Commander-in-Chief of the British forces at the beginning of the American War of Independence. He and his cousin and successor, Sir Thomas, rebuilt the house in Palladian manner with many rococo elaborate features.

Firle is a perfect example of what landscape historians describe as a 'closed village'. Such settlements, growing up on private estates, enjoy a unique status and are a vivid reminder of the autocracy of generations of powerful landowning families. The development of Firle was severely regulated and it was virtually impossible for outsiders to move into the village, which has for many years provided important employment and accommodation, operating as a self-contained community.

WALK 18 DIRECTIONS

1 Turn left out of the car park, pass the Ram Inn and follow the road round to the right, through the village of Firle. Walk along to the village stores and a footpath to Charleston. Pass the turning to Firle's Church of St Peter and continue heading southwards, out of the village.

2 Turn right at a junction of concrete tracks and make for the road. Bear left, head for the downland escarpment and begin the long climb, steep in places. On reaching the car park at the top, swing left to a gate and join the South Downs Way.

3 Head eastwards on the long distance trail and, when you reach a blue-arrowed waymarker post, turn sharp left.

WHILE YOU'RE THERE

It's always pleasing to find a church open to visitors, and many in Sussex keep their doors unlocked throughout the year. Firle church is no exception and the sign at the entrance states that the door is open from dawn to dusk. The parish refuses 'to be deterred by occasional thefts, believing it must be available to the people of the village'. There is a fee for brass rubbing, which should be paid at the village stores. The church includes a window dedicated to Henry Rainald Gage KCVO, the 6th Viscount who succeeded to the title in his 17th year in 1912 and died in 1982. The window was designed by the late John Piper and is possibly his last work in stained glass.

4 Follow the path in a north-westerly direction, down the steep slopes of the escarpment. On reaching a wooden post, where the path forks, take the lower grassy path and follow it as it descends in a wide sweep. Drop down to reach a gate and walk ahead, keeping a fence on the left. Skirt around Firle Plantation and follow the track all the way to the junction.

WHAT TO LOOK OUT FOR

In Firle's main street is the quaint old village stores. Up until motor cars began to make shopping in towns and cities easier, Firle benefited from a tailor, a bootmaker, a butcher and a baker. A blacksmith, a miller and a harness maker also operated in the village.

5 Bear left and walk along the track, keeping the dramatic escarpment on the left. As you approach the village of Firle, the track curves to the right towards the buildings of Place Farm. Cross over the junction of concrete tracks and retrace your steps back to the car park at the other end of the village.

Firle Beacon and Charleston Farmhouse

A longer walk on the downland ridge, descending to the famous country home of the Bloomsbury Set.

See map and information panel for Walk 18

DISTANCE *6 miles (9.7km)* MINIMUM TIME *3hrs 30min*
ASCENT/GRADIENT *576ft (175m)* ▲▲▲ LEVEL OF DIFFICULTY +++

WALK 19 DIRECTIONS (Walk 18 option)

To extend Walk 18 don't turn sharp left at Point 4. Instead, continue along the South Downs Way to Firle Beacon, passing a trig point. Look out for a bridleway crossing over the South Downs Way and bear left at Point A. Make for a gate and head diagonally down the downland escarpment.

Aim for a gate and skirt a belt of woodland before continuing straight on at a junction of tracks. Pass a house called Tilton Meadow and bear left at the next junction, by some barns. Follow the concrete bridleway to a right-angled bend, then swing immediately left towards Charleston Farmhouse, Point B, once the home of Duncan Grant and Clive and Vanessa Bell, members of the Bloomsbury Set. If you have time, visit the house, it includes examples of decorated furniture and murals. Look for home-made details such as the beaded lampshades, upturned pottery colanders, or a woolly fringe concealing a radiator. The walled garden is a mass of cottage planting and dense colour.

Keep ahead along the track, maintaining the outline of Firle Tower in your sights. Walk almost to the wooded corner of the field and bear left to a gate. Swing right to the next gate and continue ahead, with a close-up view of the tower. This Gothic eye-catcher was built in 1819 to accommodate the estate gamekeeper.

WHERE TO EAT AND DRINK

The Ram at Firle serves imaginative food and is a fine example of a traditional, old-style village pub. The Ram is open all day. Firle Place has a licensed restaurant serving lunches and cream teas. There is a tea terrace offering delightful views over the gardens. The café at Charleston Farmhouse serves tasty salads and sandwiches.

Cross a track, pass through trees and enter a field. Firle Place, in its lovely downland setting, can be seen from this spot. Keep to the right-hand edge of the field, soon to bear diagonally left towards some houses. Go through a wrought-iron gate by the side of a brick and flint cottage and cross the rough lane to a footpath and gate. Follow the waymarked path across the parkland, cross the main drive and follow the sign for the church. Look for a kissing gate and track and follow it to the road. Turn right and return to the car park at Firle.

Full Steam Ahead at Horsted Keynes

Recapture the golden age of steam on this glorious walk beside the Bluebell Railway.

DISTANCE *5 miles (8km)* MINIMUM TIME *2hrs*

ASCENT/GRADIENT *230ft (70m)* ▲▲▲ LEVEL OF DIFFICULTY +++

PATHS *Field and woodland paths and tracks, stretches of quiet road, 10 stiles*

LANDSCAPE *Peaceful woodland and farmland with glorious views*

SUGGESTED MAP *OS Explorer 135 Ashdown Forest*

START / FINISH *Grid reference: TQ 372293*

DOG FRIENDLINESS *Off lead on parts of Sussex Border Path. Under control in vicinity of Horsted Keynes and railway station*

PARKING *Horsted Keynes station car park. Free and open all year*

PUBLIC TOILETS *Horsted Keynes station (seasonal opening) and village*

WALK 20 DIRECTIONS

Many of us become instantly nostalgic when we think about the great days of the steam railways. There is something wonderfully evocative about the sound of an approaching steam train. Even standing on the platform of an authentically restored station and gazing fondly at the livery, the bookstalls and the adverts for seaside holidays can rekindle a host of cherished memories.

WHERE TO EAT AND DRINK

There is an excellent picnic area for fine summer days and café at Horsted Keynes station. The Green Man in Horsted has a varied menu which might include vegetarian quiche, sausages, egg and chips, and freshly carved Sussex gammon alongside tasty ploughmans' and baguettes.

Horsted Keynes station is just such a place, a railway enthusiast's dream come true. The station lies on the famous Bluebell Railway, a popular attraction since it came in to private ownership in the early 1960s. Volunteers and dedicated members of its preservation society have played a crucial role in establishing, restoring and maintaining the railway, which dates back to the early 1880s, and today Horsted Keynes station is one of the finest preserved railway stations in the country.

The restorers' intention is to recreate a sleepy Sussex junction in the years before the Second World War. Although it's essentially just a museum recalling the heyday of steam travel, the station really does have the feel of that period. It's like stepping into a time warp, where the calendar has forever been stopped at 1935.

Over the years the railway has featured in several television adverts, dramas and films. Most famously, it played a role in the television version of Edith Nesbit's *The Railway Children*, with Horsted Keynes station changing its name to Mortonhurst.

WHILE YOU'RE THERE

Make a day of it by taking a trip on the Bluebell Railway before the walk or after it. One of the most popular destinations on the line is Sheffield Park, famous for its beautiful 120-acre (49ha) garden which is situated close to the station. The garden was created with the help of 'Capability' Brown and is noted for its spring flowering rhododendrons and dazzling autumn colours.

From the car park walk up the track away from the station building, keeping the railway line on your left. Pass a footpath sign and cross the footbridge, turning right on the opposite side of the track. Follow the path as it heads away from the Bluebell Railway and crosses three stiles before quickly returning to the line. Turn left and walk alongside it to a footpath sign.

Cross the track to a stile and keep the railway on your left now. Go over two stiles, either side of a minor lane, and keep alongside the right-hand hedge boundary. Cross a stile and continue to a kissing gate. Follow the path across the pasture to the next stile and turn left by some holly trees to a footpath sign. Bear right here to the road.

Turn left for about 60yds (54m) to a stile on the right and join the Sussex Border Path. Follow the path down the field and into some woodland, crossing the rim of a pond and stream. Head up through the trees to a field, turn left and follow the path right around the field-edge and down to a gap in the vegetation and trees. Descend some steps to a footbridge and go up the slope to a kissing gate and field. Bear left and skirt the pasture to a stile and gate. Exit to the road, turn right, then left into Broadhurst Manor Road and follow the lane to the Sussex Border Path sign.

Bear right here and walk along to the entrance to Broadhurst Manor. Veer right, still on the waymarked trail, and follow the track to Broadhurst Lake, fringed by trees and covered in water lillies. Continue into Church Lane to reach the Church of St Giles.

WHAT TO LOOK OUT FOR

The lovely old Church of St Giles at Horsted Keynes is worth a look. To the right of the entrance lie the graves of former Conservative prime minister Harold Macmillan, his wife Dorothy and their son Maurice. The Macmillans lived at nearby Birch Grove.

When the lane veers right into Leighton Road, go straight on to Horsted Keynes village centre and the green. Retrace your steps down Church Lane and turn left immediately beyond a tile-hung cottage called Timbers. Go through two gates and follow a fenced path into the trees. Beyond a kissing gate, cross a track and continue on the footpath.

Go straight over at the next track, pass alongside a lake and keep left at the fork. Turn left over a footbridge at the next public footpath sign, avoid a right turning and cross two stiles to reach the road. Bear left and then turn right into Station Approach, veering right for the car park.

Pooh's Ashdown Forest

A spectacular woodland walk exploring the haunts of AA Milne's much-loved character, Winnie-the-Pooh and friends.

DISTANCE *7 miles (11.3km)* **MINIMUM TIME** *3hrs*

ASCENT/GRADIENT *170ft (55m)* ▲▲▲ **LEVEL OF DIFFICULTY** +++

PATHS *Paths and tracks across farmland and woodland, 20 stiles*

LANDSCAPE *Undulating farmland and dense woodland*

SUGGESTED MAP *OS Explorer 135 Ashdown Forest*

START / FINISH *Grid reference: TQ 473332*

DOG FRIENDLINESS *Some woodland stretches suitable for dogs off lead. On lead where notices indicate*

PARKING *Pooh car park (free), off B2026 south of Hartfield*

PUBLIC TOILETS *By village hall in Hartfield*

If as a child you were spellbound by the magic of *Winnie-the-Pooh*, then this glorious woodland walk will rekindle many happy memories of AA Milne's wonderful stories. Ashdown Forest, the real-life setting for *Winnie-the-Pooh*, represents the largest area of uncultivated land in south-east England, covering about 20 square miles (58sq km) in northern East and West Sussex. Once part of the much larger Wealden Forest, the area is now a very attractive mix of high, open heathland and oak and birch woodland scattered across the well-wooded sandstone hills of the High Weald. William Cobbett described it as 'verily the most villainously ugly spot I ever saw in England', though exploring the forest today, with its sunny glades and spacious heathland, it would be hard to agree with him.

Wild Beauty

Ashdown was a royal forest for 300 years, established by John of Gaunt in 1372. Then, it was a place of wild beauty and thick woodland, so dense in places that at one time over a dozen guides were required to lead travellers from one end to the other. After the Restoration of Charles II in 1660, large parts of the forest were enclosed and given to Royalist supporters. About 6,400 acres (2,500ha) were dedicated to the Commoners and remain freely accessible to the public. Ashdown Forest is cared for by Conservators, and today is the domain of the city dweller seeking peaceful recreation in the country. Despite this, it is still largely unspoilt.

There is much more to this place than trees. At first glance, the forest's vegetation may look rather bland but closer inspection reveals considerable variation. In the valley bottoms, wet bogs proliferate, dominated by sphagnum mosses. Round-leaved sundew, marsh clubmoss and cotton-grass also thrive in many of the bogs. The distinctive deep blue flowers of marsh gentians add a dash of colour during the autumn. The open pools are home to the nymphs of dragonflies and damselflies while the drier valley slopes are carpeted with plants such as ling, bell heather and bracken. The higher ground supports gorse and purple moor-grass.

The walk begins in a corner of Five Hundred Acre Wood – the 'Hundred Acre Wood' of AA Milne's stories. The return leg briefly follows a disused railway line before heading south across rolling countryside, passing close to Cotchford Farm, where AA Milne lived, and crossing Pooh Bridge, built in 1907 and restored in 1979. This is where Milne portrays Winnie-the-Pooh and Christopher Robin playing 'Poohsticks'.

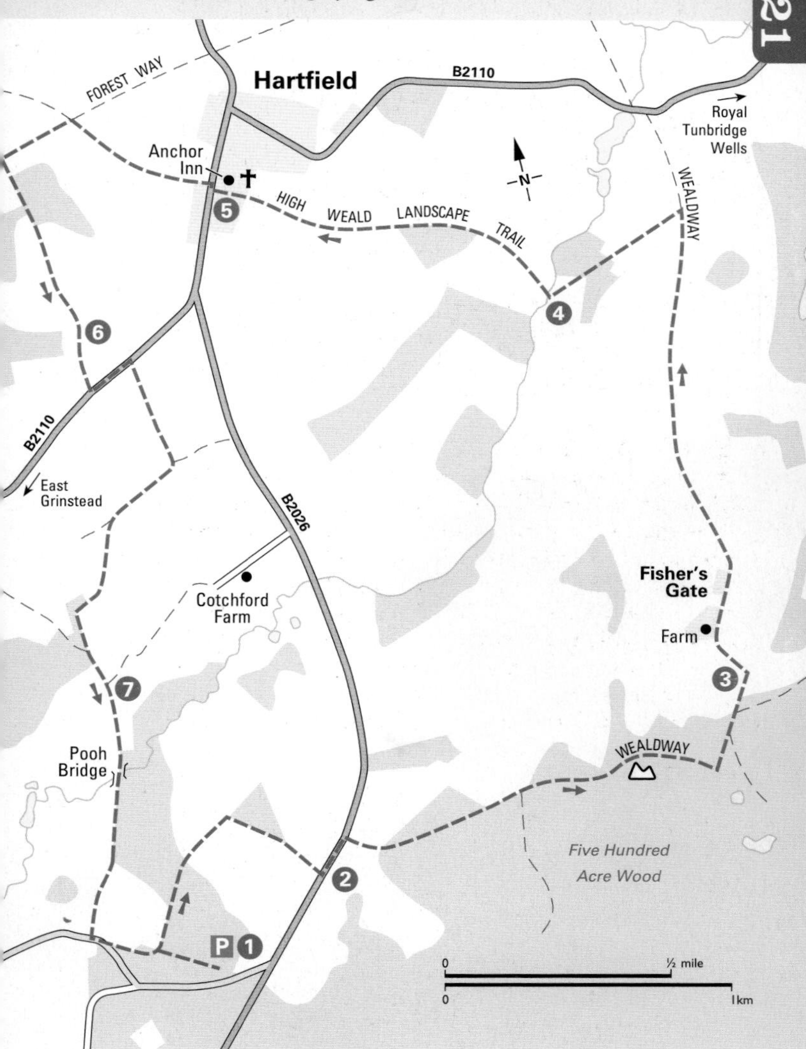

WALK 21 DIRECTIONS

❶ Follow the path signposted 'Pooh Sticks Bridge', take the third turning right and descend to a kissing gate. Cross a tree-ringed field to a kissing gate near the corner, follow the woodland path alongside fencing to a stile and then the left-hand field-edge to a track in the corner; turn right. Cross a drive to a stile and keep ahead, following the path around a paddock to a stile and the road.

Overleaf: Early morning mist over Ashdown Forest (Walk 21)

❷ Turn left, then bear right opposite The Paddocks and follow the path through Five Hundred Acre Wood to reach the Wealdway. Continue ahead, passing Kovacs Lodge. Climb quite steeply and make a wide sweep to the left. Follow the track round to the right to a fork, veer left and approach a sign for 'Fisher's Gate'.

WHERE TO EAT AND DRINK

There is a popular tea room, Piglets' in the Pooh Corner Shop, and, on the route of the walk in the village centre, is the Anchor Inn which has a varied menu with dishes such as salmon fishcakes, prawn stir-fry, and ham, egg and chips. The Haywaggon Inn also serves food and has a garden.

❸ Take the right-hand path and skirt a farm. Rejoin the drive and keep right, following the Wealdway as it cuts across undulating farmland for 0.75 mile (1.2km). Pass a turning to Buckhurst and then bear left over a stile to follow the High Weald Landscape Trail. Cross the field to a gate and stile and cut through the wood to a brick bridge.

❹ Turn right here and follow the fence, passing some paddocks. Veer right through the gateway in the field corner and make for the next field ahead. Head diagonally left across farmland to a stile. Keep to the right edge of the field to a stile, then cross a footbridge and continue by the field-edge. Turn left at a stile and enter the village of Hartfield.

❺ Bear right at the B2026, then left along the left-hand edge of a recreation ground. Cross a stile in the field corner and continue over the next stile to the Forest Way. Turn left and follow the old trackbed until you reach a gate on the left. Cross the pasture to a gate and follow the woodland bridleway. Emerging from the trees, continue to Culvers Farm.

❻ Make for the road. When you reach it turn left and walk along to the first right-hand footpath, signposted 'Pooh Bridge'. Cross the stile here and follow the clear track ahead to three further stiles before crossing a field. Follow the waymarks and make for a stile in the corner. Cross a drive to another stile and head diagonally down the field to a stile in the corner. Continue on the path and head for the next stile. Follow the lane south.

❼ When it sweeps left towards Cotchford Farm, go straight on along the public bridleway to Pooh Bridge, then follow the track as it climbs gradually alongside woodland and paddocks. Turn left at the road and when it bends around to the right, go straight ahead into the trees. Follow the footpath through the wood, back to the Pooh car park.

WHAT TO LOOK OUT FOR

Approaching the village of Hartfield, note the 700-year-old church and its ancient lychgate which includes a good example of pargeting or ornamental plasterwork. Picturesque Lych Gate Cottage is one of the oldest and smallest houses in the area. Try to find the plaque indicating an approximate date of 1520 and go into the churchyard for a better view of this lovely old building. Near by is an ancient yew tree, often found in country churchyards. The yew is thought to be a symbol of mortality and resurrection, providing protection from evil.

Classic Cuckfield

This lovely walk heads across country to sprawling Cuckfield Park, offering far-reaching views southwards to the ridge of the South Downs.

DISTANCE *5 miles (8km)* MINIMUM TIME *2hrs 30min*

ASCENT/GRADIENT *230ft (70m)* ▲▲▲ LEVEL OF DIFFICULTY +++

PATHS *Field, woodland and parkland paths, minor roads, 7 stiles*

LANDSCAPE *Rolling farmland, attractive parkland and bursts of woodland*

SUGGESTED MAP *OS Explorers 134 Crawley & Horsham, 135 Ashdown Forest*

START / FINISH *Grid reference: TQ 304246 (on Explorer 135)*

DOG FRIENDLINESS *Enclosed paths and tracks suitable for dogs off lead. On lead on farmland and busy roads*

PARKING *Free car park in Broad Street, Cuckfield*

PUBLIC TOILETS *At car park*

Standing 400ft (122m) above sea level, in the shadow of Haywards Heath, Cuckfield is one of those fortunate places that has largely escaped the threat of urban development, retaining its charm and character. It is generally thought of as a village and yet it has the feel of a classic country town that has stayed small and compact – something of a rarity in Sussex these days. It was the determination of the Sergison family back in the 19th century not to allow a railway to run across their land that saved Cuckfield from becoming yet another commuter town. The line was diverted to the east and provided the impetus for Haywards Heath instead.

Cuckoo's Clearing

Following the Norman Conquest, Cuckfield was held by the Earls Warenne and was granted a charter in 1254. The pronunciation, 'Cookfield', unusual in southern England, stems from its meaning, the delightful 'cuckoo-field'. *The Clearing where the Cuckoo Came* is also the title of a book of poetry about the village.

There are many notable buildings in the High Street and South Street, distinguished by a variety of architectural styles, but it is the famous tower and tall spire of the 15th-century Church of Holy Trinity that stands head and shoulders above the rooftops of Cuckfield. From here you can look towards the Clayton Windmills, known as Jack and Jill, high up on the South Downs.

The church, which has an unusually large churchyard, evolved from a chapel in the 13th and 14th centuries and was restored in the mid-1850s. There are various memorials and brasses inside; but the one feature which never fails to impress is the unique ceiling which boasts a 15th-century framework with moulded bosses. It is thought to have been the gift of the grandson of John of Gaunt who lived in Cuckfield in 1464. It was adorned with painted panels by a local artist in 1865.

Occa's Woodland Pasture

Outside in the churchyard, by the Church Street lychgate, is a memorial 'in proud and grateful memory of those men of the 2nd Battalion Post Office Rifles who were billeted and trained in Cuckfield between November 1914 and May 1915 before joining the batallion in France and who never returned'. The memorial was unveiled in 1968. A stone's throw from the church lies Ockenden Manor, now a hotel. The name is Old English, meaning 'Occa's woodland pasture', and for several centuries it was owned by the Burrell family who improved and extended the building.

The walk begins in the centre of Cuckfield and after passing through the churchyard, with its views of the South Downs, heads south-east, then west across country to the little village of Ansty. A narrow lane leads north to Cuckfield Park, its elegant parkland enhancing this very attractive walk.

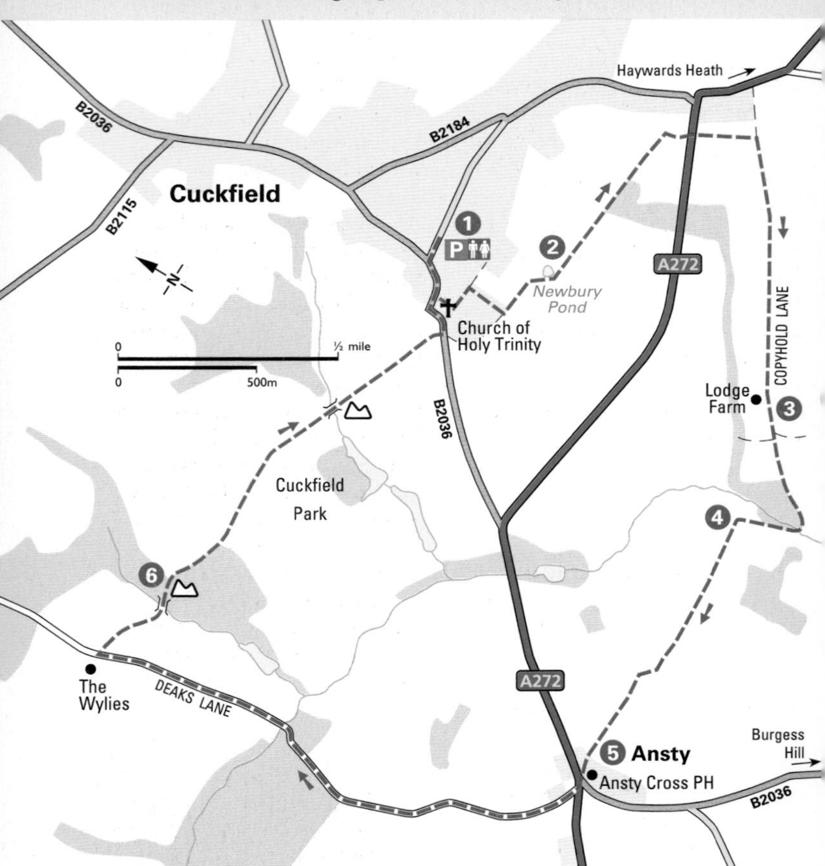

WALK 22 DIRECTIONS

1 Leave the car park by turning left into Broad Street. Bear left again when you get to the mini-roundabout and walk down to Church Street. Make for the lychgate by the parish church and go through to enter the churchyard. Head for a kissing gate on the far side, turn left and follow the track.

2 Pass Newbury Pond and cross a stile to the right of a galvanised gate. Keep to the field boundary before crossing a stile to join an enclosed path running between clumps of holly trees. Cross another stile and continue on the path until you reach a turning on the right. Follow the path down to the busy A272, cross over to a stile and follow the pretty path through the trees. Walk along to Copyhold Lane and bear right.

WHERE TO EAT AND DRINK

Cuckfield has several pubs, including the White Hart in South Street, serving hot and cold meals and bar snacks. The Ansty Cross at Ansty is mid-way round the walk and serves snacks in the bar, lunch and dinner in the restaurant.

3 Pass Lodge Farm and, when the lane swings round to the left, go straight on at the public bridleway sign, ignoring the path on the right by Copyhold Cottage. Walk ahead into the trees and follow the woodland path down to a lane. Go straight on, cross over a stream and bear right to join a footpath, quickly crossing a footbridge. Once in the field, keep to the right field-edge and make for the corner.

4 Avoid the stile here and bear left, following the field boundary and enter the next field via a gap in the hedge. Continue to skirt farmland and soon you reach a footpath sign on the bend of a track. Keep ahead, passing a house on the right, and soon you reach the A272 at Ansty.

5 Cross over and follow Bolney Road, turning right into Deaks Lane. Pass Ansty Farm and head out of the village in a northerly direction. Keep to the lane for over a mile (1.6km) and turn right opposite a house called The Wylies. Pass through a gate and follow the High Weald Landscape Trail down the field to reach a stile and footbridge.

WHAT TO LOOK OUT FOR

Cuckfield Park, established by an ironmaster in Elizabeth I's reign, was the home of the Sergison family. Later, it became a school and was open to the public. Now it is in private ownership. Keep an eye out for the striking gatehouse over to the right as you walk towards Cuckfield, which can be seen as you approach South Street.

6 Climb steeply through the woodland to reach a fence. Turn right and walk along to the fence corner by a gate. Continue ahead, merging with a grassy track to reach a galvanised gate and stile. This is the edge of Cuckfield Park. Cross a stile and follow the fenced path as it cuts between trees and carpets of bracken, dropping down to a footbridge. Ascend a steep bank to reach a stile and keep the fence on your right. Continue to a kissing gate and head towards Cuckfield's prominent church spire. On reaching South Street, turn left and return to the village centre.

WHILE YOU'RE THERE

You will identify several unexpected features in the centre of the village of Ansty. One is the Cuckfield Rural Parish Council map of rights of way in the area which shows the full route of the walk, and the village sign shows a stag watching a horse and its rider trying to climb a hilly path. Not surprisingly, the name Ansty means 'steep path to 'hilltop'.

WALK 23

Delightful Ditchling's Downs

A bracing walk exploring some of the best scenery on the South Downs.

DISTANCE *5 miles (8km)* MINIMUM TIME *2hrs 30min*
ASCENT/GRADIENT *600ft (183m)* ▲▲▲ LEVEL OF DIFFICULTY +++
PATHS *Field paths, bridleways and a stretch of road, 8 stiles*
LANDSCAPE *Downland slopes and pasture*
SUGGESTED MAP *OS Explorer 122 Brighton & Hove*
START / FINISH *Grid reference:TQ 326152*
DOG FRIENDLINESS *Off lead on enclosed paths. On lead near Ditchling*
PARKING *Free car park at rear of village hall in Ditchling*
PUBLIC TOILETS *At car park*

Ditchling is one of those picturesque villages that attracts generations of tourists and it's a popular stopping off point for walkers on the nearby South Downs Way. It shelters beneath the escarpment of the Downs, with rolling green hills and lush countryside enhancing its setting.

Attracting Artists

Over the years Ditchling's classic English village prettiness has attracted eminent figures from the world of theatre and entertainment. The 'Forces' Sweetheart', Dame Vera Lynn, settled in Ditchling; distinguished thespian Sir Donald Sinden spent his childhood here; and the actress Ellen Terry was a frequent visitor. *The Snowman* creator Raymond Briggs also lives locally.

During the early years of the 20th century Ditchling became a fashionable haunt of celebrated artists and craftsmen – among them the cartoonist Rowland Emett and the sculptor and typographer Eric Gill, both of whom moved to the village. Another member of this illustrious coterie was the calligrapher Edward Johnston, who was widely admired for his revival of the craft of formal lettering. Johnston moved to Ditchling in 1913 and lived there until his death in 1944. His most famous work is instantly recognisable to just about everyone in the country – the lettering and logo for the London Underground, distinguished by a circle with a line running through it. Simple but distinctive.

Ditchling's written records date back to AD 765. Sometime after that, the manor passed into the royal hands of Alfred the Great and Edward the Confessor. If time permits, take a leisurely stroll through Ditchling's streets and see the village at first hand. Its oldest building by far is the church, built mainly in the 13th century of local flint and imported Normandy stone. There are rare chalk carvings and a huge Norman treasure chest. During the Regency expansion of Brighton, the streets were busy with traffic en route to the resort. Horses were changed at the Bull Inn, prior to the steep pull up on to the Downs. Make a similar journey on foot and you enter a breezy world of wide skies and distant horizons.

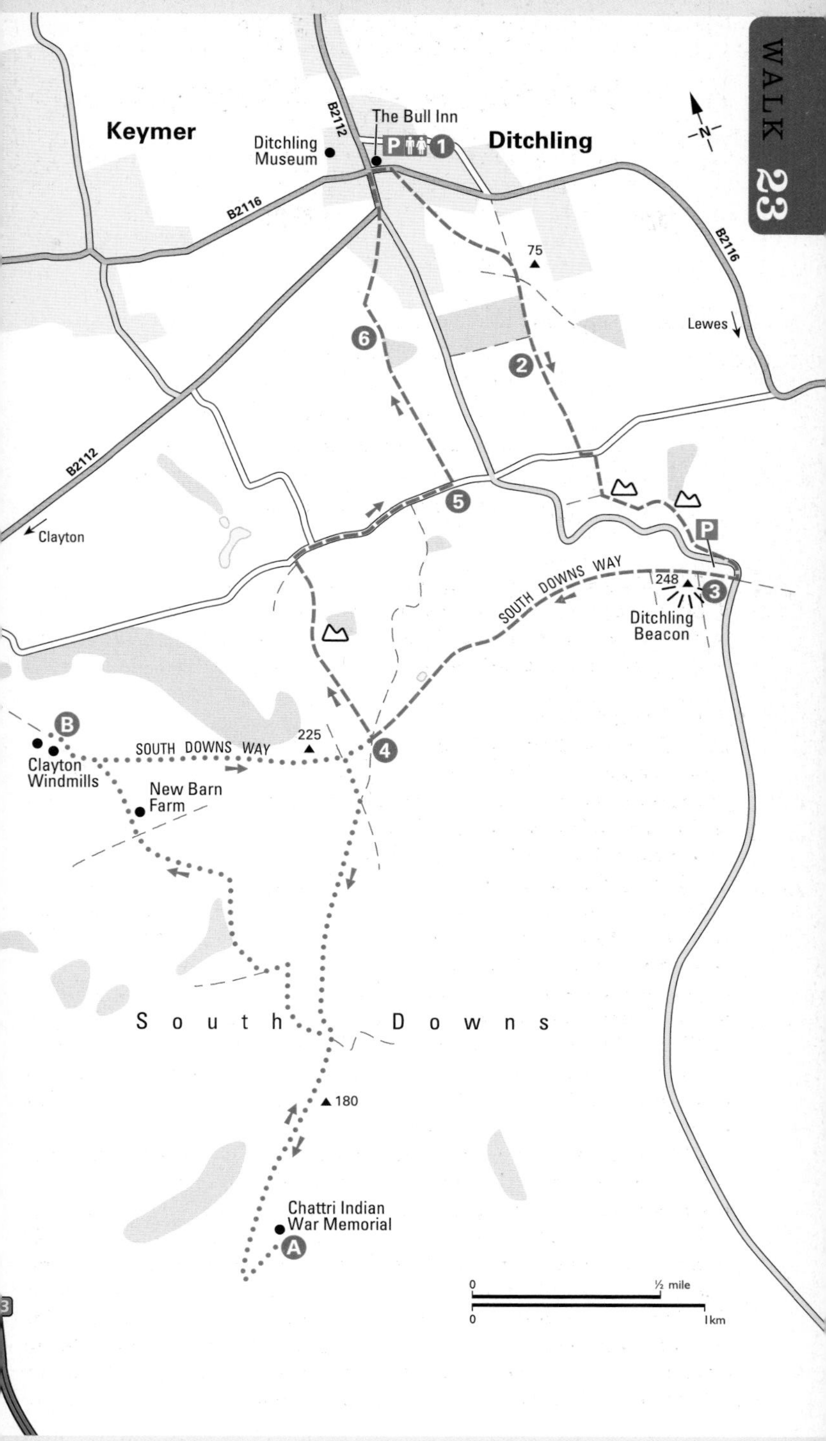
WALK 23
Keymer
Ditchling
The Bull Inn
Ditchling Museum
B2112
B2116
75
Lewes
B2112
Clayton
SOUTH DOWNS WAY
248
Ditchling Beacon
225
Clayton Windmills
New Barn Farm
South Downs
180
Chattri Indian War Memorial
0
½ mile
0
1km

WALK 23 DIRECTIONS

1 Turn right out of the car park and follow the B2116. Pass Charlton Gardens and bear right, joining a clear path signposted to the Downs. Cross four pastures via six stiles and follow a broad path running up through the woodland. Keep right at the fork by a bridleway waymark post, pass a house and go straight ahead alongside a beech hedge where a concrete track runs off right.

WHAT TO LOOK OUT FOR

Ditchling Beacon, although bleak and windswept in winter, is a delightful place. At 813ft (248m), it's the third highest point on the South Downs. The views are breathtaking and in good visibility you can see as far as the North Downs and the Ashdown Forest. Now in the care of the National Trust, the Beacon represented one of a chain of fires lit to warn of the Spanish Armada in 1588.

2 Pass Claycroft House and follow the path between trees, houses and gardens. On reaching the road, turn left and walk along to a bridleway on the right, pointing towards the South Downs Way. Follow the path, swing left at a junction and climb the steep escarpment. Keep a breathtaking view of the Weald on your left and, further up, the path runs alongside the road. Look for the South Downs Way sign ahead and turn right.

3 Pass alongside the car park and over Ditchling Beacon. Go through a gate and look for a trig point on the left. Head west along the South Downs Way, pass a dew pond and make for a major junction of paths. Keymer is signposted to the right and Brighton to the left.

4 Follow the path north towards Keymer and soon it descends quite steeply. Keep right at the fork and make for a gate leading out to a lane. Bear left to the junction, then turn immediately right past a turning for Keymer on the left. Walk towards Ditchling, then take the waymarked footpath at the next stile on the left.

5 Follow the enclosed path along the left-hand edge of the field, go through two gates by some farm buildings and make for the gate ahead. Continue ahead along the right-hand field-edge and go through a gap in the field corner.

6 Bear half left across the centre of the next field to a further gap and a waymarker post. Follow the defined path diagonally right to cross a footbridge and then a stile and follow the path out to the road. Bear left by a grassy roundabout and take the path to the right of the sign for Neville Bungalows. Cut between trees, hedges and fences, following the narrow path to the road. Bear right towards Haywards Heath and Lindfield and walk back to the centre of Ditchling, turning right into Lewes Road for the car park.

WHILE YOU'RE THERE

Visit the Ditchling Museum, situated in the old school between the church and the pond. The history of Ditchling and its artists and craftsmen is illustrated in fascinating detail. Tools, country crafts and costumes are among the displays.

Chattri War Memorial and Clayton Windmills

An extra downland loop takes in two of the area's most famous landmarks.

See map and information panel for Walk 23

DISTANCE *4.5 miles (7.2km)* MINIMUM TIME *1hr 45min (for this loop)*
ASCENT/GRADIENT *82ft (25m)* ▲▲▲ LEVEL OF DIFFICULTY +++
PATHS *Downland*

WALK 24 DIRECTIONS (Walk 23 option)

At Point 4 keep ahead on the South Downs Way for a few paces and turn left at the sign 'Path 15 Stanmer & Ditchling Beacon'. Follow the path south, cross the downland to a gate and continue across the field to the next gate where there is a path junction. Keep ahead on the same path for some time or until you spot the Chattri Indian War Memorial, Point A, unusually sited on the downland slopes.

Very atmospheric, this memorial was erected to commemorate Sikh and Hindu soldiers of the Indian Army who fought during the First World War. For those who did not survive the conflict, Brighton Corporation acquired this remote downland so that proper cremation rights could be given in accordance with their faith.

Retrace your steps to the first path junction and turn left. Follow the field boundary to a gate in the corner and head north on an enclosed path. Turn left at the next gate and follow the bridleway down the field-edge. Make for a waymark and swing right, skirting the field. Climb quite steeply beside a golf course before joining the route of the South Downs Way on a track bend.

Continue ahead and pass alongside the outbuildings of New Barn Farm. Follow the way until it turns sharp right and keep ahead towards the Clayton Windmills, Point B. Jack is a large brick-built tower mill which was worked until the early part of last century. Jill is a timber construction built at Brighton and conveyed to this site by teams of oxen in 1852. She has been carefully restored to working order.

Head back up the track, keep left at the fork and rejoin the South Downs Way. Pass the path taken earlier to the right and turn left just beyond it signed 'Keymer'. Rejoin Walk 23 at Point 4.

WHERE TO EAT AND DRINK

The Bull at Ditchling, which dates from 1560, was once a courthouse and now serves food from an imaginative menu. Ditchling Museum's coffee shop serves tea, coffee and delicious home-made cakes.

WALK 25

Doctor Brighton's Riches

A fascinating and diverse trail around one of England's newest cities.

DISTANCE *3 miles (4.8km)* MINIMUM TIME *2hrs 30min*
ASCENT/GRADIENT *164ft (50m)* ▲▲▲ LEVEL OF DIFFICULTY +++
PATHS *Pavements, streets, squares and promenade*
LANDSCAPE *The heart of Brighton and its famous seafront*
SUGGESTED MAP *Brighton street map, available at tourist information centre*
START / FINISH *Grid reference: TQ 311049*
DOG FRIENDLINESS *On lead at all times*
PARKING *Various pay car parks close to station*
PUBLIC TOILETS *Several on seafront; Royal Pavillion Gardens*

WALK 25 DIRECTIONS

Brighton began life as a small fishing village, labouring under the name of 'Brighthelmstone', but it was Dr Richard Russell who really put it on the map in 1754, when he transformed the modest settlement into one of Britain's most famous resorts. Dr Russell believed fervently in the curative properties of seawater and he began to promote Brighton as somewhere where the ailing could regain their health. The town was dubbed 'Doctor Brighton'.

The Prince Regent, who later became George IV, helped to strengthen Brighton's new-found status by moving to a farmhouse which he then transformed into the Royal Pavilion. The town's genteel Regency terraces and graceful crescents reflect his influence on Brighton.

Later still, the railway era attracted visitors and holidaymakers in their thousands, boosting the town's economy to unprecedented new heights. As a seaside town Brighton has always been a mix of 'the raucous and the refined' – as one writer described it. It's cheeky but loveable; a place of fun and excitement. In 2000 the united boroughs of Brighton and Hove were awarded city status by the Queen, one of three millennium cities to be favoured in this way.

From the front of Brighton Railway Station, keep the Queens Head on the right and walk down Queens Road. Pass Upper Gloucester Road on the right and some steps on the left. Cross over North Road and continue down to the junction with North Street. Turn left here and left again into New Road. Pass the Theatre Royal

WHILE YOU'RE THERE

Dating back to 1869, the Sea Life Centre is the largest in Britain, with many displays of live creatures. Or take a ride on the Volks Railway. Built by electrical pioneer Marcus Volk and opened in 1883, it was the first public electric railway in Britain.

WHERE TO EAT AND DRINK

With over 400 restaurants in Brighton and Hove, and countless pubs and bars, there are numerous possibilities for eating and drinking along this walk.

on the left and on the right is the Brighton Dome Pavilion Theatre. Note the striking façade of the Unitarian church. Bear right into Church Street and pass alongside the Corn Exchange, part of the Brighton Dome.

The Dome, built in 1806, was originally used as stables and a riding school for the Prince Regent. Next door to it is the exotic 18th-century Royal Pavilion, which looks stunning at night when it's floodlit. Even in the daytime, this Oriental fantasy, characterised by exuberant spires, minarets and onion domes, cannot escape your notice. The Royal Pavilion was designed by the illustrious John Nash.

Keep the Pavilion on your right, pass the George IV monument and look for three art-deco bus shelters. Cross Castle Square into Old Steine and look for the YMCA and Marlborough House on the right. Originally built for the 4th Duke of Marlborough, the house was sold in 1786 and later transformed by Robert Adam.

Turn right, signposted 'The Lanes – many of the houses here are typical of Regency Brighton – and walk along a narrow lane. Cross over East Street and look for the handsome town hall on the left, located in Bartholomews. Bear right into Market Street and pass Regent Arcade and Nile Street. Continue into Brighton Place and now you are in the district known as The Lanes. A maze of streets and narrow passages, this is the picturesque old quarter of Brighton, all that is left of 16th-century Brighthelmstone.

Veer left into Brighton Square and cross it to the right corner. Turn left into Meeting House Lane, then bear right into Union Street, noting the Bath Arms on the corner. Turn left into Ship Street, make for the seafront and look towards the old West Pier on your right.

Veer left here and then walk along to reach Brighton Palace Pier. Swing left by the Sea Life Centre and then follow Marine Parade. Pass Royal Crescent on the left and look for Bristol Court and Paston Place. Make for the steps opposite, descending to the Volks Railway.

Travel to the terminus and, if returning to the station or one of the car parks near it, alight and head for the Sea Life Centre then cross into Old Steine. Pass the Royal Pavilion and curve left into Church Street. Turn right into Regent Street, then left into North Road and on reaching the junction with Queens Road, bear right and return to the station.

WHAT TO LOOK OUT FOR

The clock tower, at the junction of Queens Road and North Street, was erected in 1888 to commemorate Queen Victoria's Jubilee the year before. The clock face has gilt Roman numerals and a gilt time-ball designed to rise and fall precisely on the hour. West Pier is one of Brighton's most famous landmarks, though it has been in a poor state of repair for some years.

WALK 26

From the Sea to the Deans

Visit a picturesque village famous for its artistic and literary associations on this exhilarating coastal and downland walk.

DISTANCE *5 miles (8km)* MINIMUM TIME *2hrs*

ASCENT/GRADIENT *305ft (92m)* ▲▲▲ LEVEL OF DIFFICULTY +++

PATHS *Busy village streets, downland paths and tracks, 6 stiles*

LANDSCAPE *Rolling downland extending to the sea*

SUGGESTED MAP *OS Explorer 122 Brighton & Hove*

START / FINISH *Grid reference: TQ 347032*

DOG FRIENDLINESS *On lead in Rottingdean. Under careful control in places*

PARKING *Free car park at Roedean Bottom, at junction of A259 and B2006*

PUBLIC TOILETS *Rottingdean village and the Undercliff*

I love seaside towns and villages and one of my favourite coastal places is Rottingdean, to the east of Brighton. I like it because it's a picturesque village with a green and lots of flint houses. But there's a stronger, more personal reason why I'm drawn to the place. My parents worked and met there, beginning their married life in this village.

Hollow Ring

Rottingdean is one of seven Saxon settlements on this stretch of the Sussex coast, all ending in 'dean.' The word 'dean' or 'dene' means hollow or valley of the South Downs. The Deans is the collective name for them and, apart from Roedean, the famous public school for girls, Rottingdean is probably the most well known. Despite expanding development over the years, the village still retains the feel of an independent community. But there's a lot more to Rottingdean than historic buildings and landmarks, as a tour of the village will reveal.

Start the walk by following the scenic Undercliff, with its close-up view of the sea, then look for a comprehensive information board at the junction of the High Street and the A259, which helps you to identify what's what and who lived where as you explore the village streets. For example, the Black Horse was said to have been a meeting place for smugglers, while Whipping Post House was the home of Captain Dunk, the local butcher and a renowned bootlegger.

Rudyard Kipling lived at The Elms in Rottingdean until driven away by inquisitive fans and autograph hunters. He wrote *Kim* and the *Just So* stories here – among other works. Kipling loved the South Downs and he found these hills a great source of inspiration. 'Our blunt, bow-headed, whale-backed Downs', he wrote in his famous poem *Sussex*.

Some of Kipling's relatives had local associations and it was here in the village that his cousin Stanley Baldwin met and married Lucy Ridsdale, whose family lived at The Dene. Baldwin was a Conservative statesman who, as Prime Minister, secured three terms in office during the 1920s and 30s. The flint church at Rottingdean is noted for its impressive stained-glass windows designed by the Pre-Raphaelite artist Sir Edward Burne-Jones, who lived at North End House on the west side of the green. Enid Bagnold who wrote the famous novel *National Velvet,* was also a local resident.

From the green, the walk climbs up to Beacon Hill above Rottingdean. The views are breathtaking as you make your way over this high ground, down to Ovingdean church and back towards Roedean.

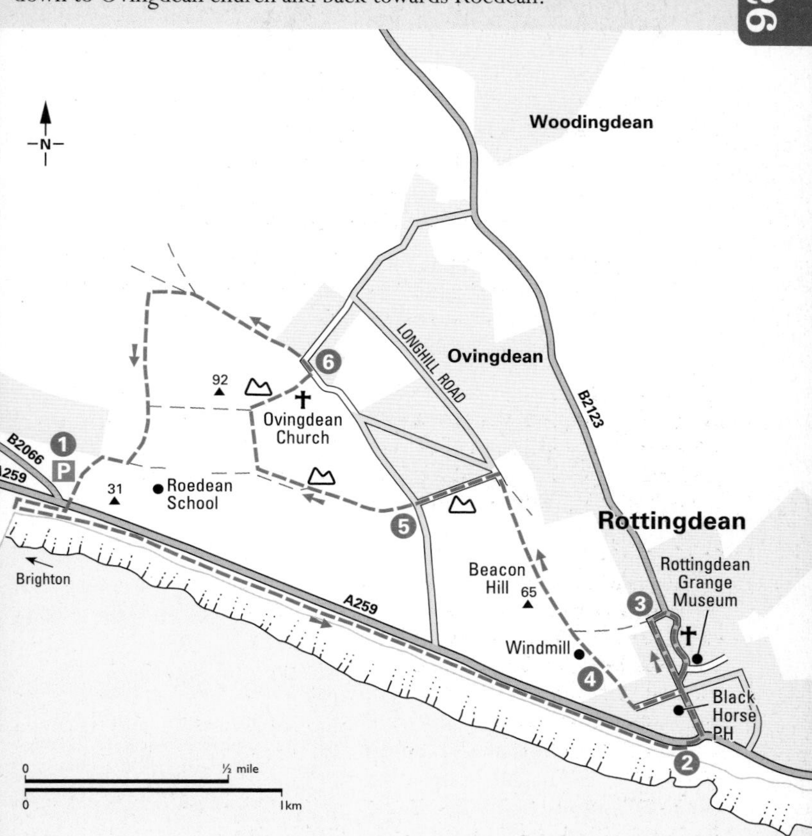

WALK 26 DIRECTIONS

1 From the car park cross the A259 and turn right towards Brighton, following the path parallel to the road. Look for the path on the left and follow it down to the Undercliff. Head east towards Rottingdean, passing a café. Continue on the path until you reach a slope and a sign for historic Rottingdean on the left.

2 Make for the village and pass the White Horse pub on the left. Cross the A259 into Rottingdean High Street. Pass the Black Horse, Nevill Road and Steyning Road and continue along the street. As you approach The Green, look for The Dene on the right.

3 Follow the road round to the right and make for the junction. Keep right and head back into

Rottingdean village. Pass the war memorial and the village pond and look for the church on the left. Pass the Plough inn and walk back down to the High Street. Turn left, then right into Nevill Road. Climb quite steeply and bear right into Sheep Walk. Look to the right here for a good view of the village and its church.

4 Keep the windmill on your left and follow the bridleway over the Downs. Woodingdean can be glimpsed in the distance and the buildings of Ovingdean are seen in the foreground. The outline of Roedean School is visible against the horizon. Continue to Longhill Road, turn left and walk down to the junction.

WHERE TO EAT AND DRINK

Along the Undercliff, you'll find a café open at weekends throughout the year. The historic Black Horse in Rottingdean is one of five inns in the village and has a snack menu which includes soup, sandwiches, ploughmans' and baguettes. Rottingdean also boasts several tea rooms.

5 Cross over to a stile and then head up the slope to a second stile in the right-hand boundary. Bear left and keep going up the hillside. Pass a private path to Roedean School and continue beside the wire fence to a stile in the field corner. Turn right and skirt the pasture to the next stile. Descend steeply towards Ovingdean church, cutting off the field corner to reach a stile. Cross into the field and keep the churchyard wall hard by you on the right.

6 Cross a stile to the lychgate and walk down to the junction. Turn left and when the road bends right, go straight on along a wide concrete track, following the

WHILE YOU'RE THERE

Visit Rottingdean Grange Museum. Originally the vicarage, the Grange used to be the home of the artist Sir William Nicholson, who lived here prior to the First World War. The building was enlarged by Sir Edwin Lutyens and now includes a gallery, museum and Tea Garden. Among the exhibits is a reconstruction of Rudyard Kipling's study. The story of the Coppers, who have done much to preserve the tradition of Sussex folksongs over the years, is also recorded. In 1950 Bob Copper traced Hilaire Belloc's journey on foot across Sussex from east to west.

bridleway. Keep left at the fork, then immediately left again at the next fork, a few paces beyond it. When the track swings quite sharply to the left, go straight on along the path. Pass a path and stile, and the car park by the A259 looms into view now. When you reach the road, by the entrance to Roedean School, cross the grass to the car park.

WHAT TO LOOK OUT FOR

As you descend to the Undercliff, look for the apartment buildings of Brighton marina. Opened in 1978, this is Europe's largest purpose-built yacht harbour, with moorings for several thousand boats. Founded in 1855, Roedean School moved to its present site in the late 1890s from Sussex Square in Brighton. During the Second World War the school relocated to Keswick in the Lake District to avoid any threat of enemy attack. At various stages along the walk there are small stones to be seen beside the path, bearing the initials RS and the date – 1938. There is no record of these stones in the school archives, though they might be some form of boundary marker.

Devil's Dyke and the World's Grandest View

A fine walk with glimpses over the most famous of all the dry chalk valleys.

DISTANCE *2.75 miles (4.4km)* MINIMUM TIME *1hr 30min*

ASCENT/GRADIENT *656ft (200m)* ▲▲▲ LEVEL OF DIFFICULTY +++

PATHS *Field and woodland paths, 7 stiles*

LANDSCAPE *Chalk grassland, steep escarpment and woodland*

SUGGESTED MAP *OS Explorer 122 Brighton & Hove*

START / FINISH *Grid reference: TQ 269112*

DOG FRIENDLINESS *Mostly off lead. On lead on approach to Poynings*

PARKING *Summer Down free car park*

PUBLIC TOILETS *By Devil's Dyke pub*

Sussex is rich in legend and folklore and the Devil and his fiendish works crop up all over the county. The local landmark of Devil's Dyke is a prime example – perfectly blending the natural beauty of the South Downs with the mystery and originality of ancient mythology. Few other fables in this part of the country seem to have caught the public imagination in quite the same way.

Disturbed by a Candle

Devil's Dyke is a geological quirk, a spectacular, steep-sided downland combe or cleft 300ft (91m) deep and half a mile (800m) long. According to legend, it was dug by the Devil as part of a trench extending to the sea. The idea was to try to flood the area with sea water and, in so doing, destroy the churches of the Weald. However, it seems the Devil might have been disturbed by a woman carrying a candle. Mistaking this for the dawn, he quickly disappeared, leaving his work unfinished. It's a charming tale but the reality of how Devil's Dyke came to be is probably a good deal less interesting. No one knows for sure how it originated, but it was most likely to have been cut by glacial meltwaters when the ground was permanently frozen in the Ice Age.

Rising to over 600ft (180m), this most famous of beauty spots is also a magnificent viewpoint where the views stretch for miles in all directions. The Clayton Windmills are visible on a clear day, as are Chanctonbury Ring, Haywards Heath and parts of the Ashdown Forest. The artist Constable described this view as the grandest in the world.

Devil's Dyke has long been a tourist honeypot. During the Victorian era and in the early part of the 20th century, the place was akin to a bustling theme park with a cable car crossing the valley and a steam railway coming up from Brighton. On Whit Monday 1893 a staggering 30,000 people visited Devil's Dyke. In 1928 HRH the Duke of York dedicated the Dyke Estate for the use of the public forever and in fine weather it can seem just as crowded as it was in Queen Victoria's day. With the car park full and the surrounding downland slopes busy with people simply taking a relaxing stroll in the sunshine, Devil's Dyke assumes the feel of a seaside resort at the height of the season. Hang-gliders swoop silently over the grassy downland like pterodactyls and kite flyers spill from their cars in search of fun and excitement. But don't let the crowds put you off. The views more than make up for the invasion of visitors, and away from the chalk slopes and the car park the walk soon heads for more peaceful surroundings.

Beginning on Summer Down, on the route of the South Downs Way, you drop down gradually to the village of Poynings where there may be time for a welcome pint at the Royal Oak. Rest and relax for as long as you can here because it's a long, steep climb to the Devil's Dyke pub. The last leg of the walk is gentle and relaxing by comparison.

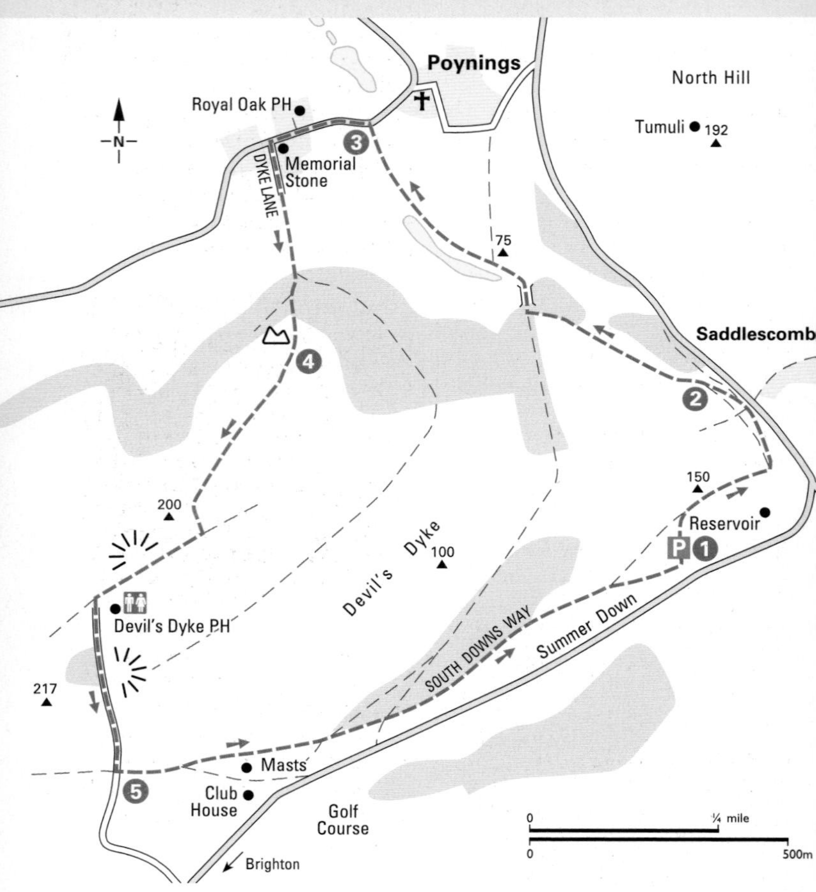

WALK 27 DIRECTIONS

1 From the Summer Down car park go through the kissing gate and then veer right. Join the South Downs Way and follow it alongside lines of trees. Soon the path curves left and drops down to the road. Part company with the South Downs Way at this point, as it crosses over to join the private road to Saddlescombe Farm, and follow the verge for about 75yds (68m). Bear left at the footpath sign and drop down the bank to a stile.

WHERE TO EAT AND DRINK

The Royal Oak located in the centre of Poynings includes a patio and gardens for warm days and offers home-cooked specialities, local seafood, cask ales and summer barbeques. The Devil's Dyke pub, three quarters of the way round the walk, has a family dining area and garden patio. Sunday lunch, baguettes and salads feature on the menu.

2 Follow the line of the tarmac lane as it curves right to reach a waymark. Leave the lane and walk ahead alongside power lines, keeping the line of trees and bushes on the right. Look for a narrow path disappearing into the vegetation and make for a stile. Drop down some steps into the woods and turn right at a junction with a bridleway. Take the path running off half left and follow it between fields and a wooded dell. Pass over a stile and continue to a stile in the left boundary. Cross a footbridge to a further stile and now turn right towards Poynings.

WHAT TO LOOK OUT FOR

Devil's Dyke consists of 183 acres (74ha) of open downland which is home to all manner of flora and fauna, including horseshoe vetch, the Pride of Sussex flower and the common spotted orchid. The adonis blue butterfly also inhabits the area. The Dyke lies within the South Downs Area of Outstanding Natural Beauty and is a designated Site of Special Scientific Interest. (SSSI).

3 Head for a gate and footpath sign and turn left at the road. Follow the parallel path along to the Royal Oak and then continue to Dyke Lane on the left. There is a memorial stone here, dedicated to the memory of George Stephen Cave Cuttress, a resident of Poynings for over 50 years, and erected by his widow. Follow the tarmac bridleway and soon it narrows to a path. On reaching the fork, by a National Trust sign for Devil's Dyke, veer right and begin climbing the steps.

4 Follow the path up to a gate and continue up the stairs. From the higher ground there are breathtaking views to the north and west. Make for a kissing gate and head up the slope towards the inn. Keep the Devil's Dyke pub on your left and take the road round to the left, passing a bridleway on the left. Follow the path parallel to the road and look to the left for a definitive view of Devil's Dyke.

WHILE YOU'RE THERE

Take a stroll through the village of Poynings, pronounced 'Punnings' locally. The village takes its name from the Poynages family, who held the manor here during the Middle Ages. Michael de Poynages, a one-time lord of the manor, left 200 marcs (£2,400) in his will towards the building of the 14th-century Church of Holy Trinity.

5 Head for the South Downs Way and turn left by a National Trust sign for Summer Down to a stile and gate. Follow the trail, keeping Devil's Dyke down to your left, and eventually you reach a stile leading into Summer Down car park.

Overleaf: View from the Fulking Escarpment (Walk 27)

Beeding's Royal Escape Route

Take a leisurely stroll through the peaceful Adur Valley to an historic bridge crossed by a fugitive king.

DISTANCE *2.5 miles (4km)* **MINIMUM TIME** *1hr 15min*

ASCENT/GRADIENT *Negligible* ▲▲▲ **LEVEL OF DIFFICULTY** +++

PATHS *Riverside, field and village paths, some road, 10 stiles*

LANDSCAPE *Adur Valley flood plain*

SUGGESTED MAP *OS Explorer 122 Brighton & Hove*

START / FINISH *Grid reference: TQ 185105*

DOG FRIENDLINESS *Take care on approach to Beeding Bridge and in Bramber*

PARKING *Free car park at Bramber Castle*

PUBLIC TOILETS *Bramber and Beeding*

Crossing Beeding Bridge, which is recorded in documents as dating back to the reign of Henry III, it is worth stopping for a few moments to consider its importance as a river crossing. Not only does the bridge play a vital part in this walk, allowing you to cross the River Adur easily from one bank to the other, but 350 years ago, in October 1651, it enabled Charles II, defeated and on the run, to escape his enemies and eventually flee to safety in France.

Pursued by Parliament

His route through the Adur Valley was one step on a long and eventful journey that has became an integral part of British history. Following the Battle of Worcester, where his army was soundly beaten, the young Charles fled across England, hotly pursued by Parliamentary forces under the leadership of Oliver Cromwell. Though documented fact, it has all the hallmarks of a classic adventure story, a colourful, rip-roaring tale of intrigue and suspense.

First, he made his way north, intending to cross the River Severn into Wales where he could find a ship and sail to the continent. But the river was heavily guarded and Charles was forced to change his plans.

Troopers on the Bridge

Instead he travelled south through the Cotswolds and the Mendips, eventually reaching Charmouth on the Dorset coast. Once again his plans to escape by boat fell through and, in a desperate attempt to avoid capture, he made his way along the South Coast to Shoreham near Brighton, where at last he found a ship which could take him to France. His journey through England lasted six weeks and during that crucial period he was loyally supported by his followers, many at great risk to their own lives.

The King's arrival in Bramber was one heart-stopping moment among many during his time on the run. As he and his escort came into the village from the west, they were horrified to find many troopers in the vicinity of the river bank. Charles realised they had been posted here to guard

Beeding Bridge, which was his only means of reaching Shoreham easily. Cautiously, he crossed the bridge and continued on his way undetected. Moments later, the Royal party looked round to see a group of cavalry hotly pursuing them across country. Charles feared the worst, but as they reached him, the soldiers suddenly overtook the King and rode off into the distance. Fortunately for Charles, they had been pursuing someone else on that occasion. After their narrow escape in the Adur valley, the group decided it was safer to split up and make their own way to the coast.

The accent is firmly on history on this very pleasant valley walk. Making for the Adur, the route follows the river to the bridge which Charles II crossed in the middle of the 17th century. The walk continues south by the river before crossing farmland back to Bamber.

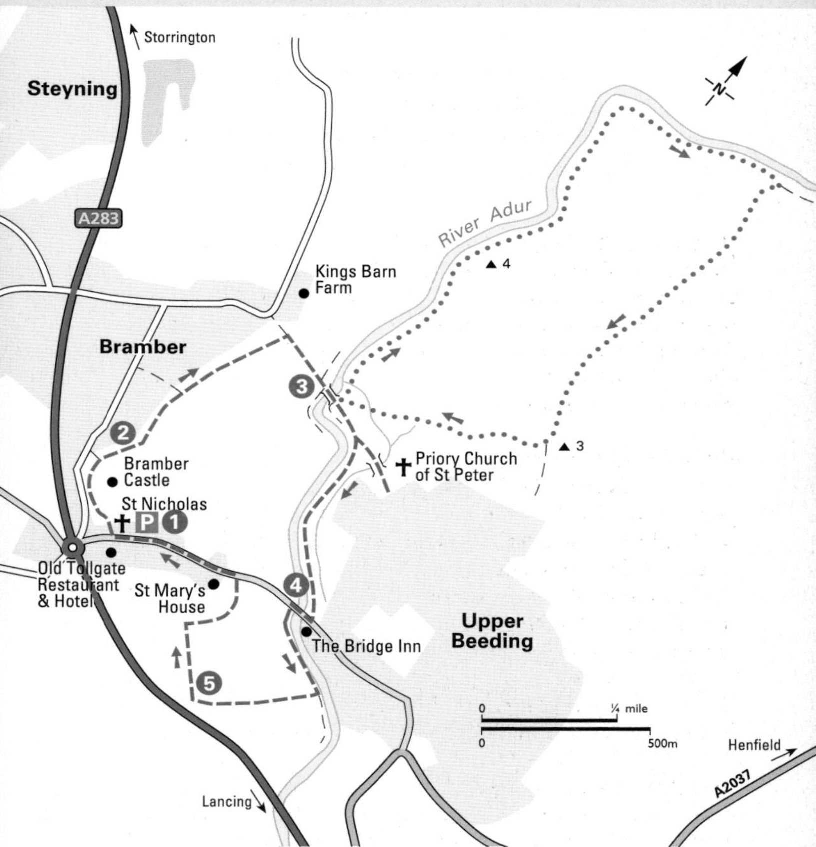

WALK 28 DIRECTIONS

1 Facing the castle and wooded ramparts, locate the narrow path in the left-hand corner of the parking area and follow it left as it meanders through the trees to the left of the castle ramparts. Keep right up the slope at a fork, then bear left downhill at the next fork to reach a track.

2 Turn right and head up through the trees, passing galvanised gates on the left and right. The rooftops of houses and bungalows peep into view along here. Continue ahead at the next signpost and the River Adur can be glimpsed between the trees on the right. Pass a footpath on the left and make for a stile ahead. Follow the grassy path to the next stile and footpath sign. Cross over and turn right towards the footbridge spanning the Adur.

3 Cross the stile and bridge. Bear right, following the river bank towards Upper Beeding. Branch off left to a footbridge and stile in order to visit the Priory Church of St Peter. Returning to the main walk, continue towards Upper Beeding. Cross a stile by a gate and continue to a kissing gate. Follow the path to the Bridge Inn at Beeding and cross the Adur.

4 Swing left and join the right-hand bank, heading downstream. Cross a stile and follow the riverside path. Continue to a right-hand stile and enter the field. Keep the fence on the right and at the fence corner go straight on, out across the field.

5 As you approach the A283, turn right in front of the stile and head towards the trees, with the ruins of Bramber Castle peeping through. Make for a stile and bear right. Follow the track as it bends left and crosses two stiles before joining a tarmac drive running through the trees to the road. Turn left, pass St Mary's House and walk along the High Street, passing the Castle Inn Hotel. On reaching the Old Tollgate Restaurant and hotel, cross the road and follow the steps up to the church and car park.

WHAT TO LOOK OUT FOR

Overlooking the Adur Valley and just off the walk is Sele Priory established by William de Braose. Sele is another name for Beeding. The vicarage now occupies the site of the old priory, part of an ancient Benedictine foundation, and next to it is the Priory Church of St Peter.

WHILE YOU'RE THERE

Before starting the walk, have a look at the ruins of Bramber Castle. Now in the care of English Heritage and the National Trust, it was built just after the Norman Conquest to defend the exposed and vulnerable Sussex coast. The castle was held by the de Braose family until 1326 when it passed to Alice de Bohun and then to her eldest son. Later, during the Civil War, it was badly assaulted by the Roundheads. Nowadays, all that remains of it is the 70ft (21m) high gateway. At the centre of the site is evidence of a motte which might have borne a timber tower. Next to Bramber Castle is the Parish Church of St Nicholas, originally the castle chapel. Like the castle, this building also suffered in battle. Cromwell's men apparently used it as a gun emplacement, causing extensive damage to the nave and tower. Towards the end of the walk, you pass the entrance to St Mary's House in Bramber. This splendid medieval building is one of the village's proudest features and the best example of late 15th-century timber framing in Sussex. One of the highlights of a tour of the house is seeing the unique printed room, decorated for the visit of Queen Elizabeth I.

Upper Beeding and Along the River Adur

A very easy extra meadowland loop takes you around the peaceful Adur Valley and into Upper Beeding.

See map and information panel for Walk 28

DISTANCE *2.5 miles (4km)* **MINIMUM TIME** *1hr 15min*

ASCENT/GRADIENT *Negligible* ▲▲▲ **LEVEL OF DIFFICULTY** +++

WALK 29 DIRECTIONS (Walk 28 option)

To extend Walk 28 and follow the River Adur a little further upstream, cross over the stile and bridge at Point 3 and then turn left. Cross five more stiles and beyond them electricity pylons can be seen marching resolutely across the landscape, with the lovely Adur sweeping dramatically to the right. Follow the river bank and make for the next galvanised gate and accompanying stile. Approach some light woodland and turn right just before it, at a fingerpost.

Head south now, with the buildings of Bramber and Upper Beeding ahead. The distinctive outline of Lancing College's vast, cathedral-like chapel and its vaulted roof of stone and chalk can be seen against the skyline. The chapel was begun in 1867 with the intention of complementing the school buildings. Work was eventually completed in 1978, after more than a century.

Veer slightly right as you steer a path across this open, low-lying ground. Make for two stiles and cross a bridge. Maintain the same direction and cross two stiles in quick succession. Walk along a reed-fringed waterway to the next stile and continue ahead, following the footpath fingerpost. Join a track and take the next footpath on the right. Go round a gate, cross over a paddock to a second gate, then cross the plank bridges and a stile to pass into the next field.

Follow the clear path back towards the Adur, with this stretch of the walk providing an unexpected view of the tower of the priory, seen peeping through the trees. Continue across the meadows, which offer a clearer impression of the site, and soon you reach the footbridge. Stay on this side of the river, turn left and follow the directions from Point 3 to Beeding Bridge.

WHERE TO EAT AND DRINK

The charming Bridge Inn at Upper Beeding is conveniently located on the route of the walk, directly beside the Adur. The pub has a good menu with traditional bar meals and snacks. Expect sandwiches, baguettes, pies and daily specials. There's also a popular beer garden.

Parham's Stately Park

Climb high up to the breezy South Downs before heading for a magnificent Elizabethan house set in beautiful parkland.

DISTANCE *5.5 miles (8.8km)* MINIMUM TIME *2hrs 30min*

ASCENT/GRADIENT *640ft (195m)* ▲▲▲ LEVEL OF DIFFICULTY +++

PATHS *Bridleways, parkland paths, and drives and stretches of road*

LANDSCAPE *Elegant parkland and steep escarpment*

SUGGESTED MAP *OS Explorer 121 Arundel & Pulborough*

START / FINISH *Grid reference: TQ 051144*

DOG FRIENDLINESS *On lead in Parham Park, in vicinity of B2139 and below Kithurst Hill car park*

PARKING *Rackham Old School free car park*

PUBLIC TOILETS *Parham Park*

WALK 30 DIRECTIONS

On leaving the car park turn right and head towards the dramatic scarp of the South Downs. Pass Rackham Road and follow the lane into the village of Rackham. Keep on the road as it cuts between fields to reach a junction. Bear left here and take care following the busy and fast B2139 for about 75yds (68m). Turn right to join a bridleway and climb steeply, passing through a gate.

Continue the steep ascent. Glancing back at intervals will reveal views of Parham Park in the distance and, away to the west, the meandering River Arun. The path curves to the right and from this high ground much of the route of the walk can be seen. Amberley, with its imposing castle remains, is also visible from this lofty vantage point. Make for a gate and join the South Downs Way.

Turn left, avoid the bridleway running off to the south, and head east. Pass a trig point on the right and continue ahead across Rackham Hill. On a clear day you can spot the sea glinting in the sunshine. Pass through a belt of trees and continue to Kithurst Hill car park on the left. Branch off here by double galvanised gates.

With the car park sign on the right, go foward to join a bridleway which initially runs parallel to the road. Follow the path to a gate, cross a pasture to a second gate and follow the path as it descends quite steeply between trees and undergrowth. Pass rows of conifers, join a track, avoiding a galvanised gate on the right, and

WHILE YOU'RE THERE

Tour the richly decorated Tudor Parham House, built during the reign of Henry VIII. The exhibition in the Ship Room shows the roles Parham played from 1922 onwards, and the restoration of the house: from fashionable country club to its role in the Second World War and later as a home for 'mentally frail old ladies'.

WHERE TO EAT AND DRINK

The Crown at Cootham offers a good selection of snacks and main meals. Rack of lamb and game casserole feature on the menu, and there are cask ales and a beer garden. Parham Park includes refreshments such as light lunches and cream teas. There is also a picnic area.

go straight on. Pass alongside a line of trees, keeping fields and downland on the right. Follow the track to reach a wooden gate leading out to the road by a house called Paygate. Turn right and then left along Clay Lane, passing Cootham Farm and Lower Barn to reach a junction with the A283. To visit Cootham and the Crown, turn right.

Walk back along the main road, avoiding Clay Lane. Make for the entrance to Parham Park, pass a stone-built lodge and go through a gate leading into the deer park. Follow the drive and when it curves gently to the left, join a waymarked parallel path on the right. Cross a pasture and look away to the south to take in a striking view of Parham House with the scarp of the Downs rising steeply behind it.

This magnificent Elizabethan mansion is one of the great treasures of Sussex, recalling the days of weekend house parties, servants below stairs and gracious living – a way of life that has all but disappeared. The wonderful setting, deer park and views of the South Downs enhance Parham's beauty and little has changed here since Tudor times. It was in 1540, at the Dissolution of the Abbey of Westminster, that Henry VIII granted the manor of Parham to Robert Palmer, a London mercer. Years later, in 1577, his great grandson, aged just two and a half, laid the foundation stone of the present larger house, which was built to incorporate the old one. The little boy's mother was a god-daughter of Elizabeth I and it is believed the Queen dined here in 1593, on her way to Cowdray from Sutton Park in Surrey. The 875-acre (354ha) estate was sold in 1601 and then again in 1922 when it was purchased by the younger son of Viscount Cowdray. The new owners opened Parham to the public for the first time in 1948 – an unusual step in the lean, post-war years. The house has been open to the public ever since and is now owned by a charitable trust.

On reaching a junction of drives, head straight on towards Rackham. Continue ahead to pass alongside a stone wall and, beyond it, a lake looms into view. Continue through the gently undulating parkland and turn left when you get to the road by West Lodges. Pass a picturesque stone house and avoid a turning to Greatham and Coldwaltham. Follow the lane down through the trees, back to the car park.

WHAT TO LOOK OUT FOR

The fallow deer here are descendants of the original herd first mentioned in 1628. The little church in the park, dedicated to St Peter, was built in 1545 and almost totally rebuilt between 1800 and 1820. Up until this time, Parham was very isolated and inaccessible, with no proper roads to enable visitors to reach the estate. The small village around the church virtually disappeared at the end of the 18th century, helping to maintain the privacy of Parham House.

WALK 31

Hilaire Belloc's Shipley

A walk around the village of a writer with a love for the Sussex countryside.

DISTANCE *7 miles (11.3km)* **MINIMUM TIME** *3hrs*

ASCENT/GRADIENT *98ft (30m)* ▲▲▲ **LEVEL OF DIFFICULTY** +++

PATHS *Field and woodland paths, country roads, 6 stiles*

LANDSCAPE *Undulating farmland and parkland*

SUGGESTED MAP *OS Explorers 121 Arundel & Pulborough, 134 Crawley & Horsham*

START / FINISH *Grid reference: TQ 144218 (on Explorer 134)*

DOG FRIENDLINESS *Off lead on drives and farm tracks. Under control near A24*

PARKING *Small free car park at Shipley*

PUBLIC TOILETS *None on route*

It has been said that Hilaire Belloc is to Sussex what Wordsworth is to the Lake District. He was certainly passionate about the county and this delightful walk suggests more than a hint of the great man's spirit.

Man of Letters

Belloc was a distinguished man of letters – a poet, writer, historian and politician in his time – and exploring the picturesque countryside surrounding his Shipley home, savouring the beauty of the landscape, you really feel that you are following in his illustrious footsteps.

He was born in France in 1870, to an English mother and a French father. After spending much of his childhood at Slindon near Arundel, Belloc served in the French artillery. He then attended Oxford University where he was an outstanding Union debater, much interested in history, politics and journalism. He forged friendships with some of the leading figures of the day and made, too, some notable enemies including Herbert Asquith, Lloyd George and HG Wells.

Belloc is best remembered as a writer of more than a hundred works. Many were inspired by his extensive travels – some of them describing extraordinary feats of endurance. He crossed the United States of America on foot to propose to a Californian girl that he had fallen in love with when he was 19 years old.

In later life he walked through France, over the Alps and down to Rome in an effort to meet the Pope. He failed due to an administrative mix-up but recorded the journey in a book, *The Path to Rome*. In 1902 he made another marathon journey walking from Robertsbridge in the east of Sussex to Harting in the west – a distance of some 90 miles (145.8km), and wrote the classic tale, *The Four Men* – a reference to himself and three fictional characters who accompany him on the journey. It is written with the passion of a man who fears that what he most loves in the world may soon fade and die.

Belloc bought King's Land in Shipley in 1906 and remained there until his death in 1953. The house was a shop when he bought it and he paid for it the princely sum of £900. The walk crosses peaceful parkland to reach the village of West Grinstead (not to be confused with the much larger East Grinstead) and then crosses the Adur to Dial Post. From here it's a pleasant country walk back to Shipley, passing Belloc's charming old windmill.

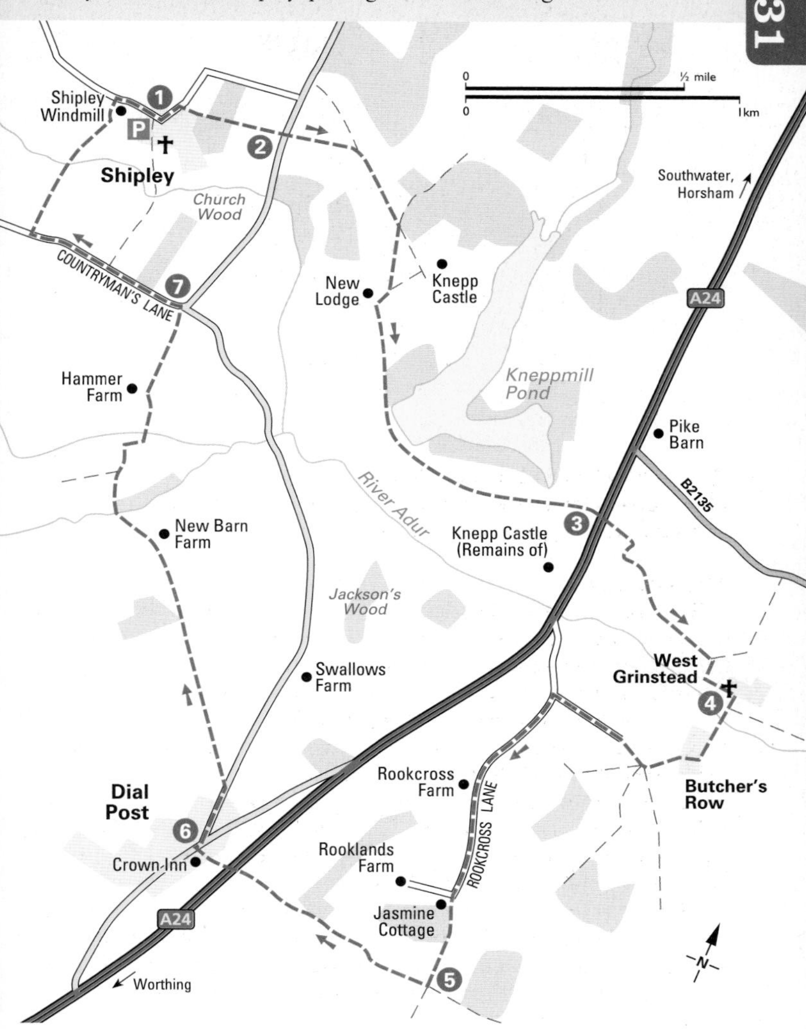

WALK 31 DIRECTIONS

1 From the car park turn right and follow the road round the left bend. After 100yds (91m) bear right through a kissing gate and follow the right-hand boundary of the field. Look for a gate into Church Wood. Follow the path through the trees to a stile and continue ahead, skirting the field. Exit to the road.

2 Cross over and follow a path through trees to a gate and enter parkland. Walk ahead to reach a footpath fingerpost. Bear right and follow the drive towards Knepp Castle. On reaching a left turning, swing right and head across the pasture. On reaching a drive, turn right and pass New Lodge. Follow the drive as it runs alongside Kneppmill Pond. The remains of the original Knepp Castle, designed by John Nash in 1809, can be seen across the fields.

WHERE TO EAT AND DRINK

The Crown at Dial Post serves good food made with locally sourced produce wherever possible. When Shipley Windmill is open, Shipley village hall serves afternoon tea and cakes.

3 Cross the A24 and look for a footpath sign and gate. Walk ahead to a footbridge in the right corner of the field. Join a woodland path and bear sharp right at the waymark. Make for a stile at the corner of the wood and skirt the field by keeping to its right edge. On reaching the hedge corner, go straight across the field for about 75yds (68m) to a footpath sign and bear right. Follow the hedge to a gate leading into the churchyard. Pass the church door and turn right at the footpath sign.

4 Make for a kissing gate situated in the corner of the churchyard and follow the paved path south. Cross the River Adur, bear left to a gate and a concrete track and continue in a southerly direction. The track becomes a tarmac drive as it passes through the hamlet of Butcher's Row. Follow it in a south-westerly direction, keeping right when you reach a junction with two tracks and a footpath. Bear left at the next junction and follow Rookcross Lane. Pass Rookcross Farm on your right, go through a gate and keep to

WHILE YOU'RE THERE

Visit Shipley Windmill, the largest in Sussex, built in 1879 and acquired by Hilaire Belloc in 1906. He called the mill 'Mrs Shipley' and used to raise his hat to it. Following Belloc's death, an appeal was launched to restore it and, since 1991, it has been in full working order.

the metalled drive for 0.5 mile (800m), passing Jasmine Cottage, before veering right at a private drive sign to Hobshorts.

5 Follow the left-hand edge of the field to a fingerpost in the first corner. Enter the next field and turn right, keeping to the field-edge. Keep to the boundary, pass some oak trees and drop down beside woodland to cross a plank bridge. Keep to the left boundary of the next field to the stile in the corner and recross the busy A24. Head for a stile and footpath sign and cross the pasture to a gateway in its left corner. Pass into the adjacent field to a bungalow and then bear immediately right. Cross over a stile to reach the Crown car park.

6 Turn right on leaving the pub, walk through Dial Post and veer left into Swallows Lane. Once clear of the village, branch off to the left and follow the straight farm road to New Barn Farm. Beyond the farm outbuildings, continue for 0.5 mile (800m) to reach the road.

7 Turn left into Countryman's Lane and pass a footpath that leads to the church. Continue onwards to the next right-hand bridleway. Follow the sheltered path to Shipley Windmill, then continue to the road and turn right for the car park.

Loxwood – London's Lost Route to the Sea

Cross pastures to discover how a forgotten canal is being brought to life.

DISTANCE *4.5 miles (7.2km)* **MINIMUM TIME** *2hrs*

ASCENT/GRADIENT *82ft (25m)* ▲▲▲ **LEVEL OF DIFFICULTY** +++

PATHS *Field paths, tracks and tow path, 4 stiles*

LANDSCAPE *Gentle farmland bisected by Wey and Arun Junction Canal*

SUGGESTED MAP *OS Explorer 134 Crawley & Horsham*

START / FINISH *Grid reference: TQ 041311*

DOG FRIENDLINESS *On lead on road and stretches of farmland*

PARKING *Free car park by Wey and Arun Junction Canal, next to Onslow Arms, Loxwood, beyond pub car park*

PUBLIC TOILETS *None on route*

The Wey and Arun Junction Canal was completed in 1816 to connect the Wey and Arun rivers and form part of a continuous inland waterway route, linking London with the south coast. Glancing at derelict stretches of the 23-mile (37km) canal today, in places either completely dried up or engulfed by weeds and and a sea of mud, you could be forgiven for thinking that 'derelict' is perhaps an understatement.

Canal Make-over

But look closer, journey along the canal tow path a little further, and you'll see that a make-over is taking place. After years of neglect, a great deal of restoration work has already been completed along the route of the old canal and a stretch beyond the Onslow Arms has now been fully restored with boat trips offered at weekends. To join together two sections either side of the B2133 here, it has been necessary to construct two new locks to take the canal underneath the modern road. But there is a great deal still to do if the Wey and Arun Canal Trust is to realise its dream of reopening this stretch of what became known as 'London's lost route to the sea'.

During the 19th century it was possible to travel by boat from London to Littlehampton on the Sussex coast via Weybridge, Guildford, Pulborough and Arundel. This route represented a tiny but important part of a once complex and extensive network of inland waterways covering England and Wales. To make that journey involved travelling along the rivers Wey and Arun which were linked between Shalford in Surrey and Pallingham in Sussex by the Wey and Arun Junction Canal.

Though the canal was initially successful, it was the arrival of the railway which spelled its demise. It finally closed in 1871, and as the years passed the waterway clogged up and was reduced to a stagnant depression in the ground, remaining in that state for the best part of a century, abandoned and largely forgotten. The lock by Devil's Hole, an abandoned oxbow of canal that was an earlier attempt to bypass a slope, was used by Canadians in the Second World War for target practice!

A Labour of Love

In the early 1970s a group of dedicated volunteers and canal enthusiasts formed the Wey and Arun Canal Trust, with the aim of restoring the canal as a public amenity, including its diverse range of wildlife habitats. Many of the original bridges and locks have been reconstructed or restored, but construction work of this kind is very expensive and every penny is needed. The conservation project depends on the Trust's fundraising efforts and the goodwill of local councils, businesses and landowners.

This pretty walk begins in Loxwood and gives an insight into the rebirth of the Wey and Arun Junction Canal, highlighting the various renovation works in progress. Heading north across lush farmland, the route eventually joins the tow path, and you'll see how the conservation programme is transforming the canal from an overgrown ditch into a vibrant waterway.

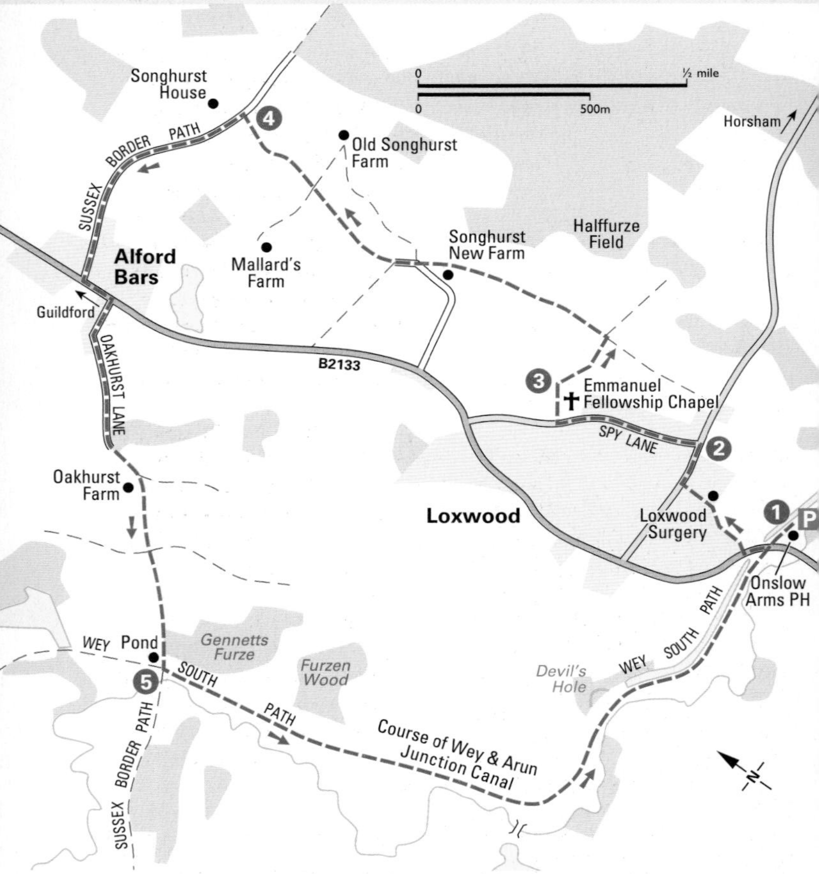

WALK 32 DIRECTIONS

1 From the car park by the Onslow Arms turn right at the B2133, cross over the canal, walk along the road for 50yds (41m) and then turn right on to a signposted path which leads between hedges. Continue walking ahead by Loxwood Surgery on the right. Turn right at the T-junction.

WHERE TO EAT AND DRINK

The Onslow Arms is characterised by its horseshoe-shaped bar. Choose from pizza, ploughmans' or sandwiches from on the main menu. There is also a beer garden and children's play area. Tanglefoot and Badger Best feature among the beers and there are usually a couple of guest ales.

2 Pass Burley Close and turn left into Spy Lane. Follow the road as it leads between houses and bungalows and look for the Emmanuel Fellowship Chapel on the right. Bear right immediately beyond the chapel, over a stile and skirt the Emmanuel Fellowship playing field.

3 Follow the path to the next stile and pass through a tongue of woodland. Make for the right-hand boundary of the field, aiming for a stile in the corner. Turn left and immediately left again by a fingerpost and stile. Follow the left-hand edge of three fields, passing Songhurst New Farm. Head for the field corner and look for a stile just to the right of a galvanised gate. Continue along a surfaced single-track lane, passing a brick-built house on the right. Continue for 0.5 mile (800m), passing a right turning to Songhurst Old Farm.

4 Turn left on reaching a T-junction with a lane, following the Sussex Border Path and pass Songhurst House. After 0.5 mile (800m), turn left at a T-junction along the right-hand verge of the B2133. Walk along to Oakhurst Lane and follow the Sussex Border Path to Oakhurst Farm. Pass between timber barns and go straight ahead when the track curves right. Follow the field path ahead into woodland and keep forward at the first T-junction, following the Sussex Border Path. Carry on to reach a pond (on the right) and a crossing of tracks.

5 Turn left here and follow the Wey South Path alongside the disused Wey and Arun Junction Canal, which here appears as an overgrown ditch on the left. Continue on the old tow path, passing through several gates. Disregard any turnings and keep to the route of the canal. Pass a lock and a footbridge and eventually you reach the B2133. Cross over, keeping to the left of the Onslow Arms and return to the car park.

WHAT TO LOOK OUT FOR

In Spy Lane is the former chapel of a religious sect formed in the 19th century. The adjoining burial ground is the final resting place of founder John Sirgood and 600 of his followers, though there are no headstones to mark their graves. Sirgood was a puritanical evangelist who came to Loxwood in 1850. He gathered around him the Society of Dependents, whose members became known as Cokelers from the name of a local field. The Cokelers carried out a great deal of charity work in the area, though they refused to solemnise marriage in their chapel, did not approve of music and books, and did not endorse sport or the theatre. The chapel is now home to the Emmanuel Fellowship, which has no connection with the extinct Cokelers.

WHILE YOU'RE THERE

Enjoy a summer afternoon cruise on the restored section of the Wey and Arun Junction Canal. The weekend trips begin by the Onslow Arms in Loxwood and last less than an hour. Longer cruises on the canal take place once a month.

WALK 33

A Downland Ramble at Amberley

Recreate the past with a visit to a working museum before climbing high on to the Downs.

DISTANCE *7 miles (11.3km)* **MINIMUM TIME** *2hrs*

ASCENT/GRADIENT *262ft (80m)* ▲▲▲ **LEVEL OF DIFFICULTY** +++

PATHS *Riverside paths, downland tracks and some roads, 2 stiles*

LANDSCAPE *Arun Valley and downland*

SUGGESTED MAP *OS Explorer 135 Ashdown Forest*

START / FINISH *Grid reference: TQ 472332*

DOG FRIENDLINESS *Off lead on stretches of downland and riverside*

PARKING *Parking by kind permission of Amberley Working Museum*

PUBLIC TOILETS *Amberley Working Museum*

It may sound strange but this invigorating downland walk begins where reality meets nostalgia. By visiting an old chalk quarry, at the start of the route, you have the chance to forget, albeit briefly, the hurly-burly of the modern world, step into the past and recall a cherished way of life that has long vanished. Amberley is a charming, tranquil village with a history going back to medieval times and was the summer residence of the Bishops of Chichester.

Amberley Working Museum

Amberley Working Museum is well worth a visit, entered via the Amberley railway station car park. The open-air museum, which covers 36 acres (15ha) originally of a long-disused chalk pit in the Arun Valley, was opened in 1979. Originally called the Chalk Pits Museum, its objective is to illustrate how the traditional industries of south-east England evolved and developed during the 19th and 20th centuries.

As well as changing its name in later years, the Amberley Museum also marketed itself as 'The Museum that Works'. And work it certainly does. Few museums thrill and excite adults and children alike as much as this one does. To prove it, there are almost 100,000 visitors a year.

Glimpses of a Past World

Visit the bus garage and the signwriter's workshop, the locomotive shed, the village blacksmith's, stop at the telephone exchange or discover the wheelwright's shop. You may meet skilled crafts people from the museum's resident team exercising ancient trades. Using traditional materials and tools, they produce a choice of fine wares which enables them to earn a living and keep their trade thriving. Elsewhere, exhibits are conserved and demonstrated by volunteers, many of whom have acquired a lifetime's experience in their trade.

One of the highlights of a visit to the Amberley Working Museum is a trip around the site on board a vintage bus, or perhaps a tour on the narrow-gauge railway. The train ride takes visitors between Amberley and

Brockham stations and yet never leaves the museum site! When you finally leave the museum, follow the River Arun and begin the gradual climb into the hills. Up here, with its wide open skies and far-ranging views, you can feel the bracing wind in your face as you explore some of the loneliest tracts of downland anywhere in Sussex.

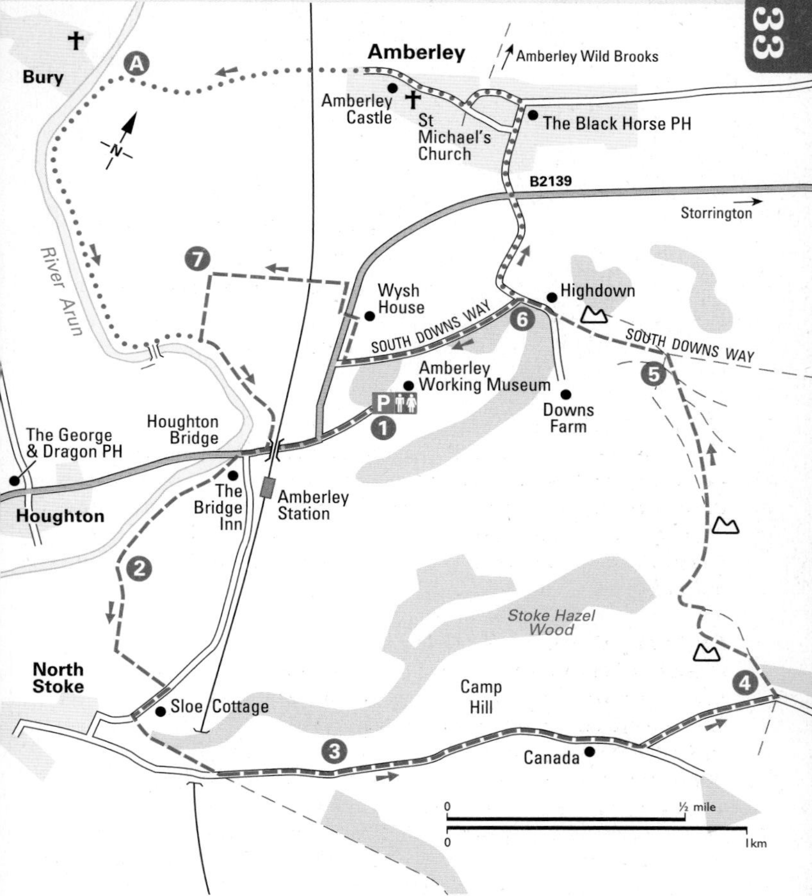

WALK 33 DIRECTIONS

1 Turn left out of the car park and pass underneath the railway bridge. Begin to cross the road bridge spanning the Arun and then bear left at the footpath sign to reach a stile by a galvanised gate. After crossing a bridge and another stile, bear right on a riverside bank to the next stile and a few paces beyond it you reach a sluice. Bear left here.

2 Follow the path between trees, turn right on reaching a lane and pass Sloe Cottage. Turn left through a gate just beyond a caravan site to join a bridleway. Follow the path as it runs above the camping ground and emerge on a track by a bridleway sign. Cross the track here and join a rough lane, turning left.

3 Stay on the lane as it climbs gradually; the Arun can be seen

below. Pass farm outbuildings and keep ahead, the lane dwindling to a track along this stretch. Veer left at the fork and follow the waymarked public right of way. Head for a signposted crossroads and turn left on a bridleway with a fence on your right.

WHERE TO EAT AND DRINK

The Bridge Inn at Houghton Bridge, close to the start of the walk, is Grade II listed and has fires and a welcoming atmosphere. Among the popular dishes are rump steak and steak and kidney pudding. Snacks include ploughmans' and sandwiches; also Sunday roasts and a children's menu. There is also a tea room at Houghton Bridge.

❹ Walk down the chalk track, pass through a gate and continue the steep descent. Look for two gates down below, set some distance apart. Cross to the right-hand gate and a reassuring bridleway sign is seen here. Follow the bridleway as it bends left, climbing steeply towards Downs Farm. Keep a fence on the left and follow the bridleway as it merges with a wide track.

❺ Keep left at the next junction and follow the South Downs Way towards the entrance to Downs Farm. Fork right at the junction, signposted 'South Downs Way' and join a narrow footpath, which begins a steep descent. Drop down the slope until you reach a tarmac lane then turn right. On the right-hand side is a prominent house called Highdown.

❻ Fork left on a lane (signposted 'The South Downs Way'). The attractions of Amberley Working Museum can be spotted down to the left. Immediately before

WHAT TO LOOK OUT FOR

A church at North Stoke, just off the route, is mentioned in the Domesday Book, though nothing here is earlier than the 13th century. The windows in both transepts have some of the most striking early tracery in southern England. From the higher ground, above North Stoke, look across the Arun Valley to the 'Alpine' spire of the church at South Stoke. On a good day you might pick out distant Arundel Castle.

the road junction, turn right and follow the South Downs Way parallel to the road. Cross the main road, continue on the other side and turn left on a concrete track over the railway line.

❼ The track turns left here in front of a metal gate and continues to the bank of the River Arun. Swing left, veering slightly away from the river bank, to join a drive and then turn left at the road. Bear right to return to Amberley Working Museum and its car park.

WHILE YOU'RE THERE

Take a look at the Arun by Houghton Bridge. This is a popular spot in the summer. A short distance away is the village of Houghton, which you might care to visit after the walk. The George and Dragon pub originally dates back to the 13th century and Charles II stopped here to take ale in October 1651, on his way to the coast after the Battle of Worcester.

Right: An authentic old bus at the Amberley Working Museum (Walk 33)

PRIZE
BEERS
BEST FOR
FASHIONS
LEA & SONS
FAMOUS THROUGH SUSSEX
WESTERN ROAD,
CD 5125
4
TARRING
DURRINGTON
HIGH SALVINGTON
LEYLAND

LDD 643E

Amberley Downs and Wild Brooks

Extend your downland ramble by heading out on to wetlands and water-meadows.

See map and information panel for Walk 33

DISTANCE *6.5 miles (10.4km)* MINIMUM TIME *3hrs*

ASCENT/GRADIENT *262ft (80m)* ▲▲▲ LEVEL OF DIFFICULTY +++

WALK 34 DIRECTIONS (Walk 33 option)

To extend Walk 34, veer right at the fork at Point ❻ and walk down to the B2139. Cross over the road into Amberley village and keep ahead at the junction in the village centre. Turn left by The Black Horse to the next road junction with a footpath opposite. Turn right, passing St Michael's Church and Amberley Castle.

The castle dates back to Norman times and was strongly fortified in 1377. Originally it was the residence of the Bishops of Chichester. However, its fate was sealed when the Parliamentarians began to dismantle it during the Civil War. Parts of the castle survive today, having been converted in to a stylish hotel. White peacocks and black swans inhabit the grounds and helicopters, ferrying guests, can sometimes be seen landing by the castle walls. The portcullis closes at midnight every night. Carry straight on.

Over to the right are glimpses of Amberley Wild Brooks, an extensive area of water-meadows that may seem to have more in common with the fenland of East Anglia than Sussex. These meadows have been designated a Site of Special Scientific Interest (SSSI) for their diversity of habitats – woodland, scrub and dry permanent pasture among them. You may spot Bewick swans and, if you're lucky, white-fronted geese. This is a popular haunt of wintering wildfowl.

Where the road ends beneath the castle wall, keep straight ahead on a path between fences. Cross two stiles, either side of the railway, and look for the spire of Bury church ahead. Follow the path to the next stile and cut across the field half left towards a footpath sign. In the second field make for a stile and bridge ahead and cross the third field in the direction signposted to the river bank and turn left, Point Ⓐ. Follow the reed-fringed Arun. Avoid the distinctive metal footbridge and keep ahead with the river on the right to return to Houghton Bridge. Bear left for the museum car park.

WHERE TO EAT AND DRINK

The Black Horse at Amberley is a popular local in the centre of the village. Good real ales and traditional pub food are available. The inn was originally several cottages and the busy village bar has a cosy atmosphere. There is also a restaurant and pleasant beer garden.

Left: Thatched cottage in Amberley village (Walks 33 and 34)

WALK 35

Getting High on Highdown Hill

A bracing hilltop walk offering classic downland views and visiting a rare chalk garden.

DISTANCE *3.25 miles (5.3km)* MINIMUM TIME *1hr 30min*
ASCENT/GRADIENT *82ft (25m)* ▲▲▲ LEVEL OF DIFFICULTY +++
PATHS *Grassy paths and well-defined bridleway, 3 stiles*
LANDSCAPE *Breezy hilltop with good views over downland and coast*
SUGGESTED MAP *OS Explorer 121 Arundel & Pulborough*
START / FINISH *Grid reference: TQ 098041*
DOG FRIENDLINESS *Highdown Hill is good for dog walking*
PARKING *Free car park and picnic area*
PUBLIC TOILETS *Highdown Gardens*

WALK 35 DIRECTIONS

Rising 269ft (81m) above the Sussex coast, Highdown Hill is a popular recreational area, a superb playground for children and a vital green lung on Worthing and Littlehampton's doorstep. Here, you can enjoy a leisurely stroll, enhanced by a wonderful sense of space and distance.

With your back to the coast, follow the path away from the car park, immediately curving left. Keep ahead on the main path until you reach a path veering off to the right to the Miller's Tomb. Pass the tomb and go through the gate to an interpretation board recording the fascinating history of Highdown Hill.

WHERE TO EAT AND DRINK

Highdown Tea Rooms, open every day throughout the year, offers rolls, sandwiches, salads, ploughmans, cakes and cream teas. Next door is Highdown Hotel, which includes two bars, a family restaurant and a carvery restaurant. Light snacks, jacket potatoes and more substantial main courses are available, as is a children's menu.

During the early part of the Iron Age there was a hill-fort on the hill, which consisted of an earthwork with a rampart and ditch. Subsequently the site was used as an Anglo-Saxon burial ground. It was discovered quite by accident in the late 19th century, when a local landowner was carrying out some tree planting inside the hill-fort. In more recent years storms uprooted and destroyed a number of trees on the site, revealing much more of the burial ground, which is thought to date from about AD 450. In 1588 a beacon was lit here to warn of the approaching Spanish Armada and during the Second World War a radar station was built on the hill.

Stride out over the hill, keeping the trees on your right. The remains of the hill-fort and its grassy earthworks can be seen now. Glancing to the right at the western end of the site, you'll identify a

WHAT TO LOOK OUT FOR

The Miller's Tomb contains the remains of John Oliver, an eccentric 18th-century miller, who, allegedly, had the tomb constructed on Highdown Hill more than 20 years before his death. The reason? So that smuggler Oliver could store contraband safely and in the least likely place. He died in 1793.

rather forlorn old triangulation pillar nestling in the grass.

Highdown Hill's grassland includes a number of important wildlife habitats. Plants most closely associated with the old chalk grazing land include cowslip, kidney vetch, chalk milkwort and common spotted orchid. The carthusian snail, a rare mollusc, has been discovered here, and birds such as linnet, goldfinch and willow warbler are known to inhabit the area.

Descend gently to a stile and gate and then go straight ahead in the next field. The stump of Ecclesden Windmill, minus its sails, can be seen in the distance. Soon the path curves to the right and hugs the field boundary, passing a track running off to the right. Maintain the same westerly direction and keep the field boundary on your right. Make for the field corner, turning left to follow the path between fences.

The old windmill lies to your right now. Continue ahead to reach a junction with a bridleway. Turn left here and then follow the path as it leads between bushes and margins of vegetation. Eventually you reach a stile on the left. Disregard it and no more than ten paces beyond the stile you arrive at a junction of bridleways.

Keep left here, avoiding the gated path on the extreme left and follow the chalky path up the slope between brambles and carpets of undergrowth. Very quickly you reach the exposed, lower slopes of Highdown Hill, following its contours in an easterly direction. Avoid the paths running up over the hill and where there are two parallel routes ahead, keep to the right-hand lower path.

On reaching a waymark, keep ahead towards trees, pass the Miller's Tomb on the left and then retrace your outward steps back to the car park.

WHILE YOU'RE THERE

Visit Highdown's lovely chalk garden, which is open throughout the year and was established by Sir Frederick and Lady Stern, who worked for 50 years to prove that plants would grow on chalk. The garden was created out of a disused chalk pit at a time when horticulturalists were travelling to China and the Himalayan regions to collect rare and beautiful plants. Many of the original species from those early expeditions survive in the garden today. Following Sir Frederick's death in 1967, his widow left the garden to Worthing Borough Council.

WALK 36

Climping – Where Countryside Meets Coast

The last surviving stretch of undeveloped coast between Bognor Regis and Brighton forms the backdrop to this fascinating walk.

DISTANCE *4 miles (6.4km)* **MINIMUM TIME** *2hrs*

ASCENT/GRADIENT *Negligible* ▲▲▲ **LEVEL OF DIFFICULTY** +++

PATHS *Field paths, roads and stretches of beach, 1 stile*

LANDSCAPE *Sandy beaches, open farmland and riverside development*

SUGGESTED MAP *OS Explorer 121 Arundel & Pulborough*

START / FINISH *Grid reference: TQ 005007*

DOG FRIENDLINESS *Off lead on enclosed paths and beach area. Under control near the Arun and on road at Climping*

PARKING *Car park at Climping Beach*

PUBLIC TOILETS *Climping Beach*

Much of the Sussex coast has grown and evolved since early pioneering photographers captured classic seaside scenes at Worthing, Hove and Littlehampton, and now a chain of urban development extends almost continuously from Bognor to Brighton. Here and there are still hints of the coastline as it used to be before the builders moved in, but Climping Beach, where this walk begins, is an altogether different place. There is a welcome feeling of space and distance here, rarely experienced on the Sussex coast.

Remote Spot

One of Climping's main attractions is its remoteness. It is approached along a country lane which terminates at the beach car park. A glance at a map of this area might cause some confusion. The village of Climping, which has a 13th-century church, lies a mile (1.6km) or so inland and the nearest settlement to Climping Beach is Atherington. The medieval church and various dwellings of this old parish now lie beneath the sea, which has steadily encroached upon the land, and all that is now left of low-lying Atherington are several houses and a hotel.

Climping Beach, together with neighbouring West Beach, is popular with holidaymakers as well as locals who want to enjoy the space. The National Trust protects more than 2 miles (3.2km) of coastline here. The low-water, sandy beach is backed by shingle banks which, in places, support vegetation, a rare habitat in Britain. In addition, there are active sand dunes, which are another rare and fragile feature of the coastline. Only six areas of active sand dunes survive on the south coast between Cornwall and Kent and three of them are in Sussex.

After crossing a broad expanse of flat farmland, the walk eventually reaches the River Arun, opposite Littlehampton. From here it's a pleasant amble to West Beach, finishing with a spectacular stroll by the sea, back to Climping Beach. There is much to divert the attention along the way, but it is this lonely stretch of coastline that makes the greatest impression – a vivid reminder of how the entire West Sussex coast once looked.

WALK 36 DIRECTIONS

1 From the beach car park take the road leading away from the sea, passing the entrance to Bailiffscourt Hotel on the left-hand side. Continue walking along the road until you reach the Black Horse Inn and take the next footpath on the right, by some thatched cottages.

2 When the track swings left, continue ahead across the field to a signpost, in line with a distant blue building, at a junction with a byway. Go straight over and follow the path through the fields.

3 By some derelict outbuildings, join a track on a bend and turn right. As it swings right, take the signposted path and begin by following the boundary hedge. Stride out across the field, cross the concrete footbridge and bear left at the footpath sign to follow a deep ditch known as the Ryebank Rife. When the path veers away from the ditch, cross the field to a line of trees, aiming towards a distant blue storage tower. There is a stile to cross here, followed by a footbridge.

4 Turn right and walk along the road to a turning on the right for

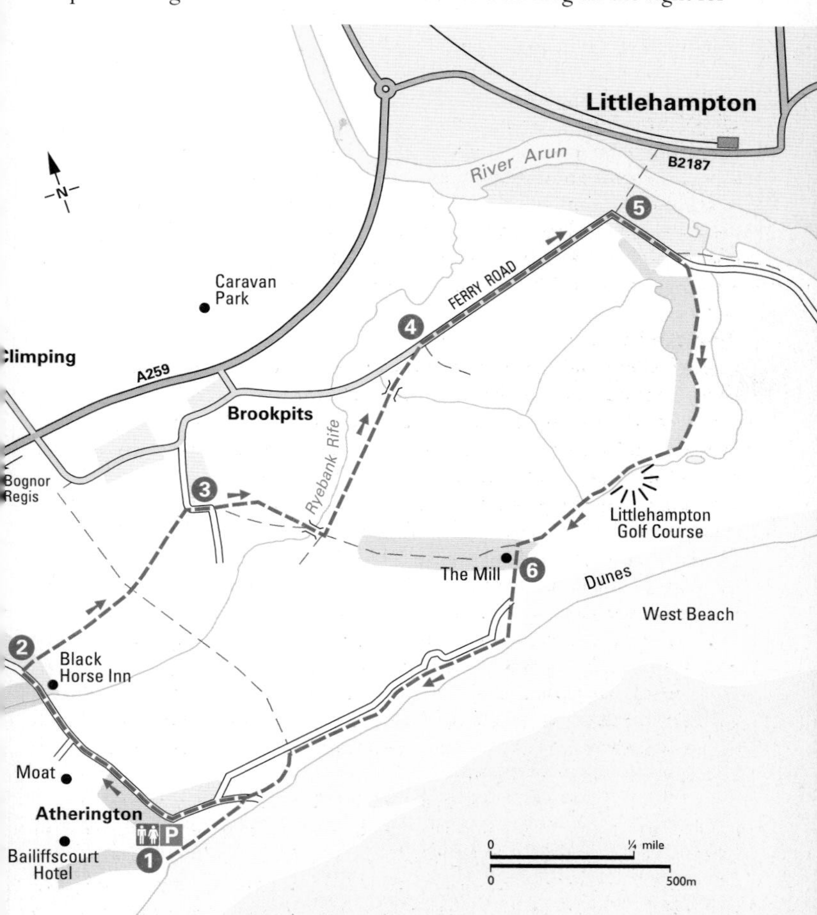

WHAT TO LOOK OUT FOR

As you begin the walk look for the entrance to Bailiffscourt Hotel. Roger de Montgomery, William the Conqueror's cousin, permitted Benedictine monks from the Abbey of Seez to establish a chapel at Climping. Their bailiff occupied what is now the hotel. The building was later remodelled in the authentic medieval style.

Littlehampton Golf Club. The walk follows this road, but before taking it, continue ahead for a few steps to have a look at the footbridge crossing the Arun. The buildings of Littlehampton can be seen on the far side and, if time allows, you may like to extend the walk by visiting the town.

5 Continuing the main walk, follow the road towards West Beach and the golf club, veering right at a car park sign to follow an enclosed path to a kissing gate and briefly cross the golf course to enter a wood. The path runs along a raised bank and later emerges into the open with good views over this unspoilt coastal plain. Keep to the path and at the end of the golf course you reach a house known as The Mill. Avoid the path on the right here and keep left.

6 Continue walking along the footpath and soon it reaches West Beach. Look for the interpretation board which explains how this open stretch of coastline has been shaped and influenced by climatic conditions and the sea over the centuries. Follow the footpath sign towards Climping, skirting the edge of the beach and avoiding a byway on the right as you approach the beach car park.

WHERE TO EAT AND DRINK

The Black Horse Inn near Climping Beach is located on the route of the walk and is an ideal stop if you're completing it on a summer's evening. Eat and drink outside or relax in the cosy bar. The inn offers a range of ales and a wide selection of hot and cold food. Littlehampton has a good choice of pubs, including several in the vicinity of the Arun.

WHILE YOU'RE THERE

Read about the history of the bridge over the Arun. The river, which is fast flowing and reaches up to 7 knots during the spring tides, effectively separates the town of Littlehampton from the adjoining countryside. The view downstream from the bridge is of various boatyards and Docklands-style warehouses which have been converted into apartments. Littlehampton was a thriving port during the Middle Ages when stone from Normandy was landed here for the construction of many of the county's churches and castles. Later, it became a fashionable seaside resort with its seafront lined by striking Victorian and Edwardian villas.

Standing Guard Over Arundel

A very varied walk following the River Arun to Arundel Park and concluding with a tour of this handsome Sussex town.

DISTANCE *3.25 miles (5.3km)* MINIMUM TIME *2hrs*
ASCENT/GRADIENT *197ft (60m)* ▲▲▲ LEVEL OF DIFFICULTY +++
PATHS *Riverside and parkland paths, some road walking, 2 stiles*
LANDSCAPE *Valley, rolling parkland and town*
SUGGESTED MAP *OS Explorer 121 Arundel & Pulborough*
START / FINISH *Grid reference: TQ 020071*
DOG FRIENDLINESS *Off lead on tow path. Not permitted in Arundel Park. Final stage of the walk is along busy roads in Arundel*
PARKING *Mill Road fee-paying car park, Arundel*
PUBLIC TOILETS *Arundel town centre and Swanbourne Lake*
NOTE *Arundel Park is closed annually on 24th March*

Arundel has rows of elegant Georgian and Victorian buildings, fine shops and a picturesque riverside setting, but topping the list of attractions is surely the town's magnificent castle – the jewel in Arundel's crown. As you drive along the A27 to the south of Arundel, the great battlemented castle, together with the grandiose French Gothic-style Roman Catholic cathedral, can be seen standing guard over the town, dwarfing all the other buildings in sight.

Norfolk House

There has been a castle here since the 11th century, though most of the present fortification is Victorian. Arundel Castle is the principal ancestral home of the Dukes of Norfolk, formerly the Earls of Arundel. There are various family portraits inside the castle, some of them believed to date back to the Wars of the Roses. The Norfolks have lived at Arundel since the 16th century. According to the plaque at the bottom of the High Street: 'Since William Rose and Harold fell, There have been Earls at Arundel'.

The castle was attacked by Parliamentary forces during the Civil War. However, it was extensively rebuilt and restored in the 18th and 19th centuries. Within its great walls lies a treasure trove of sumptuous riches, including a fascinating collection of fine furniture dating from the 16th century, tapestries, clocks and portraits by Van Dyck, Gainsborough, Reynolds, Mytens and Lawrence – among others. Personal items belonging to Mary, Queen of Scots and an assortment of religious and heraldic items from the Duke of Norfolk's collection can also be viewed.

The walk starts down by the Arun and from here there are teasing glimpses of the castle, but it is not until you have virtually finished the walk that you reach its main entrance, saving the best until last. Following the river bank through the tranquil Arun valley, renowned for its bird life, the walk eventually reaches Arundel Park, a delight in any season. Swanbourne Lake, a great attraction for young children, lies by the entrance to the park, making it easily accessible for everyone. However, once the bustling lake scene fades from view and the sound of children at play finally dies, the park assumes a totally different character. Rolling hills and tree-clad slopes crowd in from every direction and only occasional serious walkers, some of them following the long distance Monarch's Way recreational path, are likely to be seen in these more remote surroundings.

You may feel isolated, briefly cut off the from the rest of the world at this point, but the interlude is soon over when you find yourself back in Arundel. Pass the huge edifice of the cathedral, built in 1870, and make your way down to the castle entrance. Walk down the High Street, said to be the steepest in England, and by the bridge at the bottom you can see the remains of the Blackfriars monastery, dissolved in 1546 by Henry VIII.

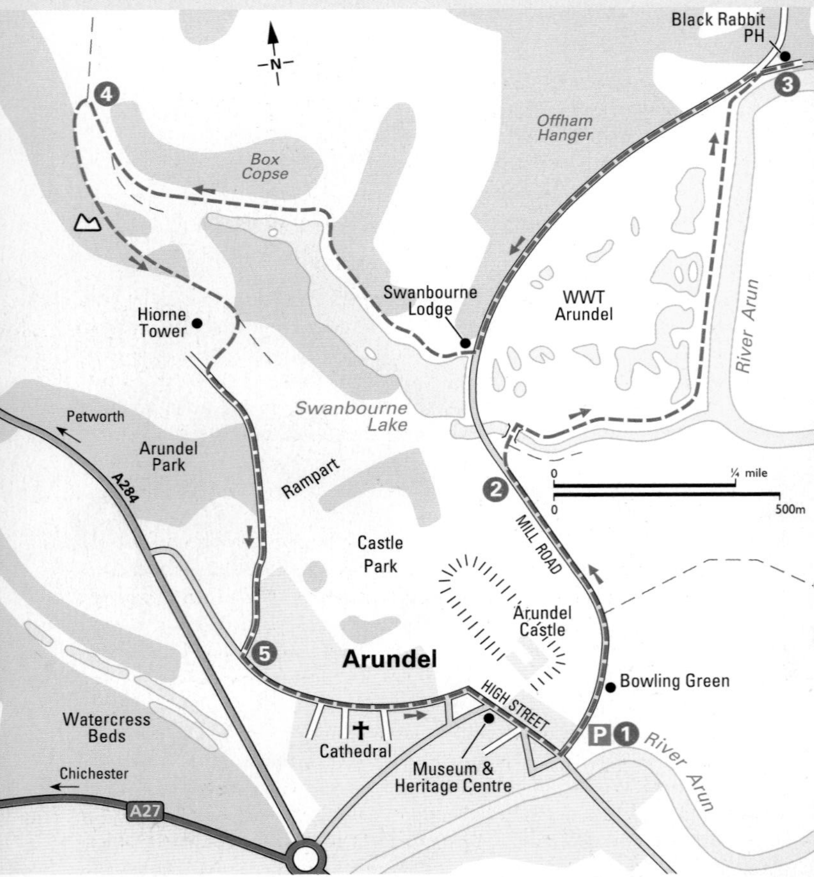

WALK 37 DIRECTIONS

❶ From the car park in Mill Road, turn right and walk along the tree-lined pavement. Pass the bowling green and a glance to your left will reveal a dramatic view of historic Arundel Castle with its imposing battlements.

❷ Follow the road to the elegant stone bridge, avoid the first path on the right and cross over via a footbridge and turn right to join

WHERE TO EAT AND DRINK

Arundel offers a good choice of places to eat and drink. The Black Rabbit at Offham, on the route of the walk, is delightfully situated on the Arun. Cheerful hanging baskets add plenty of colour in summer when you can sit outside and relax in these very attractive surroundings. The WWT Arundel Wetland Centre offers a café by the water's edge and there is a picnic site by Swanbourne Lake.

the riverside path, partly shaded by overhanging trees. Emerging from the trees, the path cuts across lush, low-lying ground to reach the western bank of the Arun. Turn left here and walk beside the reed-fringed Arun to the Black Rabbit pub, which can be seen standing out against a curtain of trees.

❸ From the Black Rabbit, turn left on the minor road back towards Arundel, passing the entrance to the WWT Arundel Wetland Centre. Make for the gate leading into Arundel Park and follow the path alongside Swanbourne Lake. Eventually the lake fades from view as the walk reaches deeper into the park. Ignore a turning branching off to the left, just before a gate and stile, and follow the path as it curves gently to the right.

WHILE YOU'RE THERE

Visit the Wildfowl and Wetlands Trust Conservation Centre, which is situated directly on the route of the walk. There are many attractions to divert your attention. Ducks, geese and swans from all over the world make their home here and the popular boardwalk enables you to explore one of the largest reed beds in Sussex. There's also an award-winning visitor centre. Call in at the Arundel Museum and Heritage Centre which illustrates the town's colourful and lively past with a series of fascinating exhibits and photographs, providing a unique glimpse into the development of the town and the lives of its people. The museum, in the High Street, has examples of costume, weaponry and demonstrations of local industries such as brick and pipe making.

WHAT TO LOOK OUT FOR

Climbing up from Arundel Park brings you to Hiorne Tower, a remote but beautifully situated folly. Triangular in plan and recently restored, the folly was built by Francis Hiorne in an effort to ingratiate himself with the then Duke of Norfolk so that he might work on the restoration of Arundel Castle. The duke agreed to engage him on the restoration but Hiorne died before he could begin work.

❹ Turn sharply to the left at the next waymarked junction and begin a fairly steep ascent, with the footpath through the park seen curving away down to the left, back towards the lake. This stretch of the walk offers glorious views over elegant Arundel Park. Head for a stile and gate, then bear immediately right up the bank. Cross the grass, following the waymarks and keeping to the left of Hiorne Tower. On reaching a driveway, turn left and walk down to Park Lodge. Keep to the right by the private drive and make for the road.

❺ Turn left, pass Arundel Cathedral and bear left at the road junction by the entrance to Arundel Castle. Go down the hill, back into the centre of Arundel. You'll find Mill Road at the bottom of the High Street.

Overleaf: Arundel Castle and the River Arun (Walk 37)

TOPAZ

Treasures in Trust on the Slindon Estate

Tour and explore a sprawling National Trust estate on this glorious woodland walk which offers fine views of Sussex.

DISTANCE *4 miles (6.4km)* **MINIMUM TIME** *2hrs*

ASCENT/GRADIENT *82ft (25m)* ▲▲▲ **LEVEL OF DIFFICULTY** +++

PATHS *Woodland, downland paths and tracks, 4 stiles*

LANDSCAPE *Sweeping downland and woodland*

SUGGESTED MAP *OS Explorer 121 Arundel & Pulborough*

START / FINISH *Grid reference: SU 960076*

DOG FRIENDLINESS *Unless signed otherwise, off lead, except in Slindon village*

PARKING *Free National Trust car park in Park Lane, Slindon*

PUBLIC TOILETS *None on route*

It all began in 1895, the year the National Trust was founded by three far-sighted, visionary Victorians whose objective was to acquire sites of historic interest and natural beauty for the benefit of the nation.

Trust in Future Generations

The Trust has come a long way since those early, pioneering days. More than 100 years after its foundation, it is the country's biggest landowner, depending on donations and legacies and the annual subscriptions of its two million members for much of its income. The statistics are awesome. Over the years it has acquired 600,000 acres (243,000ha) of countryside, much of which is freely open to everyone, 550 miles (891km) of coastline, over 300 historic houses and more than 150 gardens, all of which it aims to preserve and protect for future generations. It is some achievement.

Slindon Estate

Much of the West Sussex village of Slindon is part of the National Trust's 3,500-acre (1,419ha) Slindon Estate, which is situated on the southern slopes of the South Downs between Arundel and Chichester. The estate, the setting for this lovely walk, was originally designed and developed as an integrated community and it is the Trust's aim to maintain this structure as far as possible.

Take a stroll through Slindon village as you end the walk and you can see that many of the cottages are built of brick and flint, materials typical of chalk country. During the medieval period, long before the National Trust was established, Slindon was an important estate of the Archbishops of Canterbury. Even earlier it was home to Neolithic people who settled at Barkhale, a hilltop site at its northern end.

Downland Scenery

As well as the village, the estate consists of a large expanse of sweeping downland dissected by dry valleys, a folly, several farms and a stretch of Roman road. Glorious hanging beechwoods on the scarp enhance the picture, attracting walkers and naturalists in search of peace and solitude. Parts of the estate were damaged in the storms of 1987 and 1990, though the woods are regenerating, with saplings and woodland plants flourishing in the lighter glades. Typical ground plants of the beechwoods include bluebell, dog's mercury, greater butterfly orchid and wood sedge.

To help celebrate its centenary in 1995, the National Trust chose the Slindon Estate to launch its 100 Paths Project, a scheme designed to enhance access to its countryside properties by creating or improving paths. This glorious, unspoiled landscape offers many miles of footpaths and bridleways, making it an excellent choice for a country walk.

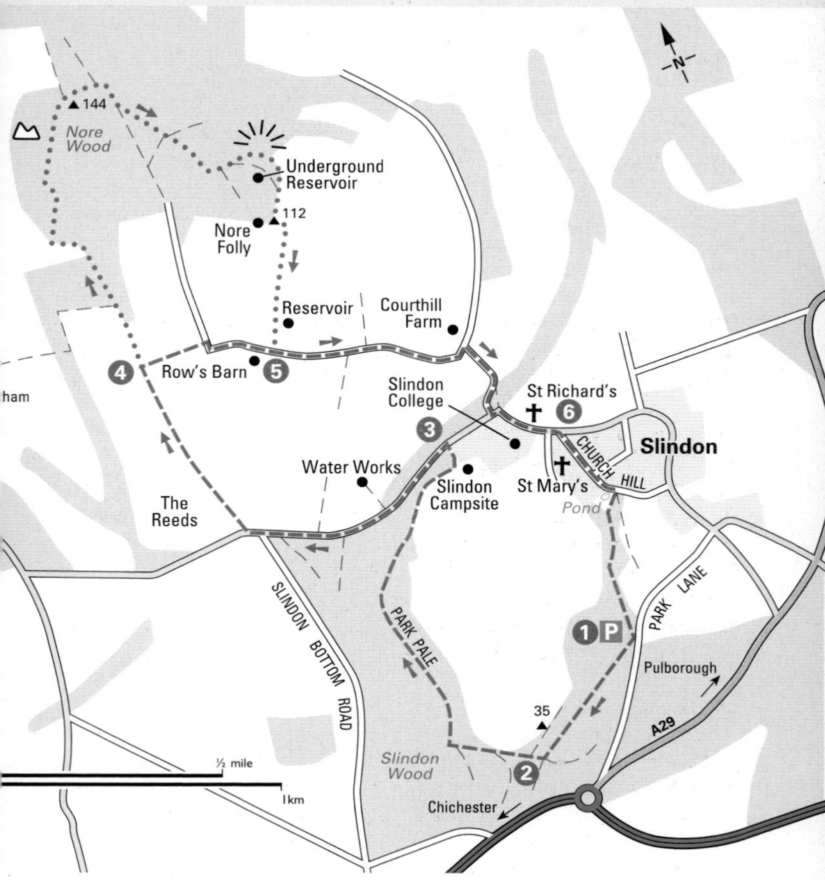

WALK 38 DIRECTIONS

❶ From the car park walk towards the road and turn right at a 'No riding' sign, passing through the gate to join a wide straight path cutting between trees and bracken. The path runs alongside sunny glades and clearings and between lines of attrative beech and silver birch trees before reaching a crossroads.

❷ Turn right to a second crossroads and continue ahead here, keeping the grassy bank and ditch, all that remains of the Park Pale, on your right. Follow the broad path as it begins a wide curve to the right and the boundary ditch is still visible here, running parallel to the path. On reaching a kissing gate, continue ahead, soon skirting fields. As you approach the entrance to Slindon campsite, swing left and follow the track down to the road.

3 Turn left and follow the road through the woodland. Pass Slindon Bottom Road and turn right after a few paces to join a bridleway. Follow the path as it cuts between fields and look for a path on the right.

4 Cross the stile, go down the field, up the other side to the next stile and join a track. Turn right and follow it as it immediately bends left. Walk along to Row's Barn and continue ahead on the track. Nore folly (See Walk 39) can be seen over to the left.

5 Continue straight ahead along the track, following it down to some double gates and a stile. Pass to the right of Courthill Farm, turn right and follow the lane or soon branch left on to a parallel woodland path to the next road. Bear left and pass Slindon College on the right and St Richard's Catholic Church on the left before reaching Church Hill.

6 Fork right into Church Hill, pass the church and make for the pond, a familiar weeping willow reaching down to the water's edge. Look for mallard ducks here. Turn right around the far end of the pond on the obvious waterside path to enter the wood. On reaching a fork, by a National Trust sign for the Slindon Estate, keep left and walk through the trees, to return to the car park.

WHERE TO EAT AND DRINK

The George Inn at Eartham (off the route by 0.75 mile/1.2km) has a choice of food, with pasta, pies and rice dishes, as well as steaks. The bar and dining room area are open plan and there is a secluded beer garden.

WHAT TO LOOK OUT FOR

As you stroll through peaceful Slindon Wood, at the start of the walk, look for the remains of the medieval Park Pale, more commonly described as a bank and ditch. This was originally designed to protect the park's deer. In palaeolithic times, the sea extended this far inland – hard to believe now as you look at the wooded surroundings.

A preserved shingle beach indicates that the sea was once 130ft (40m) higher than it is today. Courthill Farm, towards the end of the walk, was once the home of the French-born writer Hilaire Belloc and his wife when they were first married. He spent part of his childhood in the village (See Walk 31).

WHILE YOU'RE THERE

Have a look at the Church of St Mary, which is partly Norman and greatly restored. Inside is a rare wooden effigy to Sir Anthony St Leger who died in 1539. Slindon House, now part of a college, was one of the rest-houses of the Archbishops of Canterbury during the Middle Ages.

Slindon Estate and Out to Nore Folly

A longer walk through the Slindon Estate's characteristic cool woodlands to an 18th-century hunting lodge.

See map and information panel for Walk 38

DISTANCE *5.75 miles (9.3km)* MINIMUM TIME *2hrs 45min*

ASCENT/GRADIENT *210ft (64m)* ▲▲▲ LEVEL OF DIFFICULTY +++

PATHS *Hanging beechwoods and remote downland, 6 stiles*

WALK 39 DIRECTIONS (Walk 38 option)

It's well worth extending Walk 38 if you've got the time. The woodland stretches, through glorious beechwoods, are deliciously cool on a baking hot summer day and the views throughout the walk over rural Sussex are really outstanding.

Don't turn right at the stile at Point 4; instead go straight on along the bridleway, heading north. Avoid a turning for Eartham on the left, pass a bridleway sign and follow the path as it begins to climb quite steeply between the trees. On the higher ground the bridleway starts to widen, picking its way through extensive woodland.

Descend to a junction and turn right. Follow the track between trees, veering right at the first fork following the yellow arrow and 100yds (91m) later fork left through a wooden barrier. Continue through the woodland to a junction, with the boundaries of an underground reservoir partly visible on the right. Go forward through a galvanised gate and, as you emerge from the extensive tree cover, you may well want to stop for a moment to enjoy the breathtaking view of the coast, including the white tent-like structure of Butlins at Bognor Regis and, to the right, the Isle of Wight and Chichester Cathedral. Walk ahead, following the track down to the trig point.

Previously seen from a distance, Nore Folly suddenly looms large beside you. Built for the Countess of Newburgh, reputedly as a copy of an Italian archway she had seen in a print, the 18th-century folly was later enlarged for use as a shooting lodge. The National Trust carried out extensive repair work in 1973 and today the brick and flint archway still stands.

Turn left here, cross the stile and follow the grassy path to the next stile. Bear right and keep close to the field boundary, with the stony track closely parallel to the right. Cross three stiles to reach a track and turn left, rejoining Walk 38 to follow Points 5 and 6 returning to the car park.

Around Bignor's Roman Remains

A villa, illustrating the talent and enterprise of the Romano-British people, lies close to the start of this superb downland walk.

DISTANCE *5.25 miles (8.5km)* **MINIMUM TIME** *2hrs*

ASCENT/GRADIENT *773ft (235m)* ▲▲▲ **LEVEL OF DIFFICULTY** +++

PATHS *Downland and woodland tracks and paths, some road*

LANDSCAPE *Rolling countryside and well-wooded slopes*

SUGGESTED MAP *OS Explorer 121 Arundel & Pulborough*

START / FINISH *Grid reference: SU 974128*

DOG FRIENDLINESS *Quiet lanes with little traffic. Parts of walk follow tracks and paths where dogs can run free*

PARKING *Bignor Hill free car park*

PUBLIC TOILETS *Bignor Villa – open March to October*

WALK 40 DIRECTIONS

From the lofty vantage point of Bignor Hill, which rises to 737ft (25m) and is cared for by the National Trust, follow the tarmac lane down towards Bignor Roman Villa. There are classic views between the trees over extensive Sussex landscape. The lane descends through the woodland, passing a bridleway on the right as it bends left. On reaching Bignor village, take the road signposted 'Sutton and Duncton'. Pass a telephone box and on the right is picturesque Yeoman's House. To visit the Roman Villa, one of the largest in Britain, turn right here and walk along to the entrance.

Discovered by a ploughman in 1811, Bignor features various mosaics which are considered to be among the finest in the country, depicting scenes of gladiators and representations of Venus and Medusa. Originally the villa consisted of about 70 buildings situated in a walled enclosure of over 4 acres (1.6ha). The entire estate may have extended to about 200 acres (81ha), confirming that a wealthy or influential person would have lived here, possibly the equivalent of a modern aristocrat. Construction of the building was probably started around the end of the 2nd century AD and it may well have been occupied for at least 200 years.

To resume the walk, retrace your steps to Yeoman's House and continue ahead along the road. The road bends left and passes the Parish Church of Holy Cross.

WHAT TO LOOK OUT FOR

Near the end of the walk is a charming dew pond, one of a number to be found on the South Downs. Originally used for watering sheep before there was piped water and troughs, these traditional ponds are important wildlife habitats as well as a classic feature of the landscape. Dew ponds really owe their name to folklore. The vast majority of the water that fills them comes from rainfall.

WHERE TO EAT AND DRINK

Bignor Roman Villa includes a free picnic area for visitors and a cafeteria providing tea, coffee and light snacks. The White Horse pub at Sutton lies at the foot of the South Downs, directly on the route of the walk. There is a good choice of imaginative food and a selection of popular beers.

A yew tree, so familiar to country churchyards, can be seen in the corner. Follow the lane, ignoring a left turn, as it descends steeply through the trees and then climbs between high hedges towards Sutton. Pass the village sign and follow the road as it bends left by a bridleway running off to the right. Walk into the village. When the road bends right by the White Horse, go straight on towards Barlavington and Duncton.

Follow the lane between stone-built houses and cottages and head out of the village. Keep left at the fork and follow the 'No through road'. A tree-clad scarp, the walk's next objective, looms ahead. When the lane bends left, fork right on the bridleway. Further on, the track can become wet and muddy underfoot, at the point where you share the route with a stream. You reach drier ground soon enough. Begin a gentle, slow ascent through the woodland and gradually the path narrows and becomes progressively steeper. The dramatic ascent eases further up and here you avoid a left-hand footpath. Soon daylight can be seen ahead, reaching through the trees. At a meeting point of tracks, go forward and then bear left after about 30yds (27m). A gate can be seen here, leading into a field on the right. Follow the chalk track as it climbs gently, with far-ranging views over remote, well-wooded country. The track curves towards several transmitters which can be seen peeping above the trees.

Pass a National Trust sign for Bignor Hill and a bridleway on the right. Keep forward through woodland and now the track begins a gentle descent. Gradually the views widen to reveal glorious woodland and downland stretching into the distance. Head down to a junction, keep ahead on the South Downs Way and avoid the signposted route to Gumber Bothy. Shortly the car park comes into view ahead.

WHILE YOU'RE THERE

Pause to appreciate the landscape and history of the South Downs near Bignor. There is strong evidence of the Roman occupation here and running across Bignor Hill is Stane Street, a Roman road constructed about AD 70 to connect the port of Chichester with London. The National Trust owns several miles of it. You pass a section of the road at the end of the walk at the signpost to 'Gumber Bothy'.

Good Going at Glorious Goodwood

One of Britain's best known racecourses lies beside this woodland walk which includes an optional spur to the Weald and Downland Open Air Museum.

DISTANCE *3.5 miles (5.7km)* **MINIMUM TIME** *1hr 30min*

ASCENT/GRADIENT *328ft (100m)* ▲▲▲ **LEVEL OF DIFFICULTY** +++

PATHS *Woodland tracks and field paths, section of Monarch's Way and one lengthy stretch of quiet road, 4 stiles*

LANDSCAPE *Mixture of dense woodland and scenic downland*

SUGGESTED MAP *OS Explorer 120 Chichester, South Harting & Selsey or 121 Arundel & Pulborough*

START / FINISH *Grid reference: SU 897113 (on Explorer 120)*

DOG FRIENDLINESS *Can run free on woodland tracks*

PARKING *Counter's Gate free car park and picnic area at Goodwood Country Park or large free car park opposite racecourse*

PUBLIC TOILETS *Weald and Downland Open Air Museum*

Think of horse racing on the South Downs and you immediately think of Goodwood, without doubt one of Britain's loveliest and most famous racecourses. The course rises and falls around a natural amphitheatre, with the horses dashing along the ridge to create one of the greatest spectacles in the racing world. Its superb position, high on the Downs, amid magnificent beechwoods, draws crowds from far and wide, and for one week every summer it becomes 'Glorious Goodwood' when thousands of racegoers travel to Sussex to attend one of the most prestigious events of the sporting and social calendar. According to *The Times*, Goodwood is '*the* place to be and to be seen'.

Unfortunate Reputation

The course opened in 1801 after the Duke of Richmond gave part of his estate, Goodwood Park, to establish a track where members of the Goodwood Hunt Club and officers of the Sussex Militia could attend meetings. However, Goodwood's track record has not always been unblemished. Towards the end of the 19th century the racecourse acquired a rather unfortunate reputation in the area when the rector of nearby Singleton protested to the Chief Constable in the strongest terms over the rowdy behaviour of racegoers. As a result, the crowds were restrained.

Hunt with Tradition

The walk begins at Goodwood Country Park, a popular amenity area characterised by woodland and downland grass, and initially follows part of the Monarch's Way through extensive woodland, down to the village of East Dean. Along the road is neighbouring Charlton, famous for the Charlton Hunt. Established in the 18th century, the hunt's most memorable chase took place on 28th January 1738, beginning before eight that morning and not finishing until nearly six that evening. Many of those taking part were from the elite, upper ranks of society and for ten hours that day a fox led the pack a merry dance in the surrounding fields and woods. Eventually, the hounds cornered their prey, an elderly vixen, near the River Arun.

If time allows, you may want to extend the walk at this point and visit the Weald and Downland Museum, with its unusual collection of traditional homes and workplaces in both village and countryside. The main walk finishes by skirting Goodwood and on race days crowds line the bridleway alongside it, watching as camera crews dash back and forth in an effort to capture the best television images. The sound of the PA system floats across the course as you witness all the colourful activity.

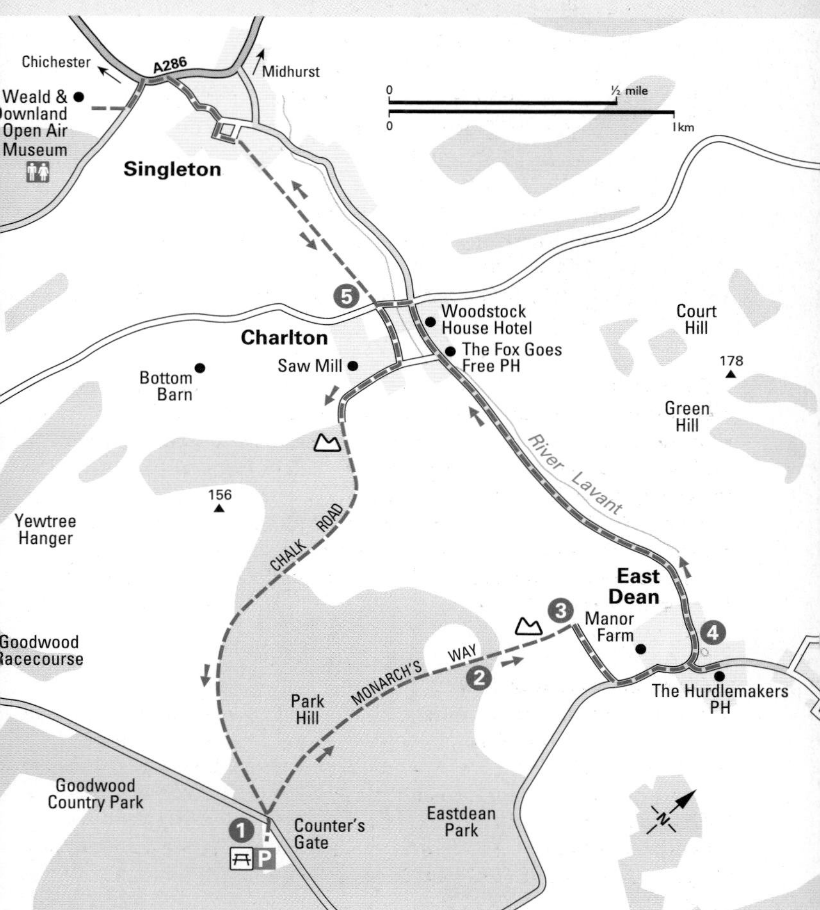

WALK 41 DIRECTIONS

1 Make for the western end of Counter's Gate car park and look for a footpath sign by an opening leading out to the road. Cross over to a junction of two clear tracks, with a path on the right. Follow the right-hand track, which is signposted 'public footpath' and part of the Monarch's Way, to a gate and stile. Continue to the next gate and stile and then cross a clearing in the woods.

❷ Cut through this remote, thickly wooded country, following the gently curving path over the grassy, plant-strewn ground and down between trees to reach a gateway. The village of East Dean can be seen nestling down below. Head diagonally right down the steep field slope to reach a stile in the corner.

WHAT TO LOOK OUT FOR

The village of East Dean, with its pond and ancient cottages of Sussex flint, is one of the prettiest in the area. For many years it was a thriving centre for hurdlemaking, and before the First World War seven craftsmen operated here. The village inn, formerly the Star and Garter, is now called The Hurdlemakers.

❸ Cross into the adjacent field and follow the boundary to a second stile leading out to the road. Bear left and walk down into East Dean, passing Manor Farm. Keep right at the junction in the village centre and, if it's opening time, follow the road towards Petworth in order to visit The Hurdlemakers pub.

❹ Leave East Dean by keeping the pond on your right-hand side and follow the road towards Midhurst and Singleton.

WHERE TO EAT AND DRINK

The Hurdlemakers at East Dean and the 400-year-old Fox Goes Free at Charlton both offer a good range of meals and snacks and enjoy a very pleasant South Downs setting. There is a café at the Weald and Downland Open Air Museum, offering hot soup, filled rolls, quiche, Cornish pasties and various cakes and pastries made with flour from the local working watermill.

On reaching Charlton village, pass The Fox Goes Free pub and the Woodstock House Hotel and take the next left turning. Follow the lane to a stile on the right and a turning on the left. To visit the Open Air Museum at Singleton, cross over into the fields and follow the straight path. Return to this stile by the same route and take the road opposite.

❺ Walk along to the junction and turn right by the war memorial, dedicated to fallen comrades of the Sussex Yeomanry in both World Wars. Follow Chalk Road which dwindles to a track on the outskirts of Charlton. Once clear of the village, the track climbs steadily between the trees. On the left are glimpses of a glorious rolling landscape, while to the right Goodwood's superb downland racecourse edges into view between the trees. Follow the track all the way to the road and cross over to return to the Counter's Gate car park.

WHILE YOU'RE THERE

Visit the Weald and Downland Open Air Museum which includes many attractions. Set in 50 acres (20ha) of lovely Sussex countryside, the museum offers a fascinating collection of over 40 regional historic buildings which have been saved from destruction, painstakingly restored and rebuilt in their original form. You can discover Victorian labourers' cottages, visit a recreated Tudor farmstead and explore ancient building techniques in the museum's hands-on gallery.

Meandering Around Midhurst

A host of delights awaits on this town and country walk, which follows the pretty River Rother to the ruins of Cowdray House.

DISTANCE *3 miles (4.8km)* **MINIMUM TIME** *2hrs*
ASCENT/GRADIENT *123ft (37m)* ▲▲▲ **LEVEL OF DIFFICULTY** +++
PATHS *Pavements, field, riverside tracks and country road, 4 stiles*
LANDSCAPE *Midhurst town and its beautiful rural setting on the Rother*
SUGGESTED MAP *OS Explorer 120 Chichester, South Harting & Selsey*
START / FINISH *Grid reference: SU 886217*
DOG FRIENDLINESS *Off lead on tracks and stretches of riverside. On lead on roads and busy streets in Midhurst town centre*
PARKING *Car park by tourist information centre in North Street*
PUBLIC TOILETS *Car park and elsewhere in Midhurst*

Midhurst is one of those classic Sussex towns crying out to be discovered and explored on foot. Many splendid buildings and a wealth of history add to its charm and character. HG Wells attended school at Midhurst and wrote: 'I found something very agreeable and picturesque in its clean and cobbled streets, its odd turnings and abrupt corners, and in the pleasant park that crowds up one side of the town'. Midhurst became the model for Wimblehurst in his book *Tono Bungay*.

Estate Yellow

Look around you on this walk and you'll spot the vivid yellow paintwork of houses owned by the Cowdray Estate. The grounds of Cowdray Park are famous for polo matches – an important part of the sporting calendar. Not so well known are the majestic ruins of Cowdray House, seen from the car park at the start of the walk and visited just before you finish it. The house, built for the Earl of Southampton, dates back to about 1530 but was largely destroyed by fire in 1793. However, the shell survives and you can see around the Great Chamber, the Great Parlour and the Chapel.

Begin the walk by embarking on a town trail. It's an easy stroll through the old market town of Midhurst with plenty to see along the way. Old photographs of the town taken in the early part of the 20th century show the part-16th-century Angel Hotel and the building which now houses Barclays Bank. The famous tile-hung library has been preserved too, and the medieval interior is certainly worth looking at. Built in the early part of the 16th century, the building was thought originally to have been a storehouse or granary. This part of Midhurst is known as Knockhundred Row. The delightfully evocative name is thought to date back to the time when Midhurst had a castle, and the owner could exercise his right to summon 100 men to defend the castle by knocking on the doors of 100 households in the town.

The road passes the old chemist shop where HG Wells worked before attending Midhurst Grammar School. His mother was housekeeper at nearby Uppark House. In the middle of the street, flanked by striking houses and shop fronts, lies the town's war memorial on which the names of several regiments are recorded. Follow the road to the imposing Parish Church of St Mary Magdalen and St Denys, which is mostly 19th century but with earlier traces.

The walk, ideal for a summer's evening, eventually leaves Midhurst and heads for rolling, wooded countryside. But it's not long before you are returning to the town, following a path running through woodland above the Rother. Here you can step between the trees on the right to look down at the river and across to Cowdray House. This vista is one of the highlights of the walk, a moment to savour on the homeward leg. The walk finishes by following the Queen's Path, a favourite walk of Elizabeth I.

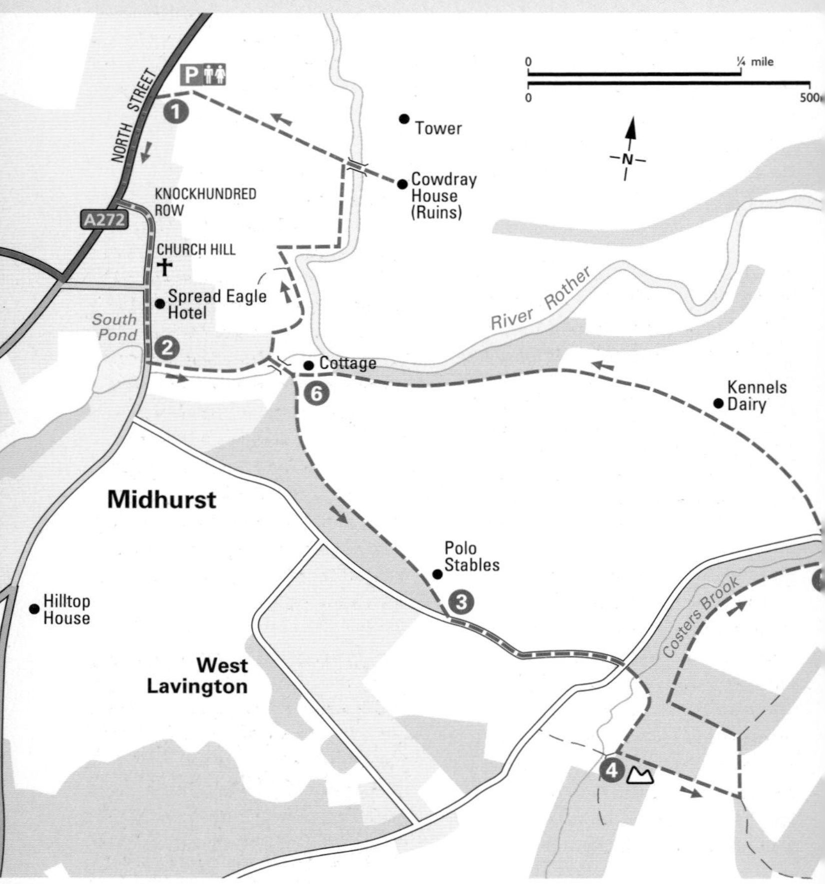

WALK 42 DIRECTIONS

❶ From the car park by the tourist information centre turn left and walk along North Street, passing the post office. Bear left into Knockhundred Row. Walk along Church Hill and into South Street to pass along the side of the historic Spread Eagle Hotel.

❷ Turn left by South Pond into The Wharf, following a bridleway beside industrial buildings and flats. Trees on the right enclose a stream. Bear right at the next waymarked junction, cross the bridge and pass a cottage on the left. Keep the wooden fencing on the right and avoid the path running off to the left. Make for a stile, then continue ahead along the edge of fields, keeping trees and vegetation on the right. Cross two stiles and follow the path to the right of the polo stables.

3 Keep left and follow a pleasantly wooded stretch of road. Pass some pretty cottages and on reaching a bend join a bridle path signposted 'Heyshott and Graffham'. Follow the track as it curves to the right.

WHILE YOU'RE THERE

Have a look at St Ann's Hill, just off the route of the walk, above the River Rother. This natural mound was once the site of a fortified Norman castle, though all that remains of it today are a few stones amid this grassy knoll. Information panels explain the history of the site in some detail.

4 Veer left just before the entrance to a house and follow the waymarked path as it climbs quite steeply through the trees, passing between woodland glades and carpets of bracken. Drop down the slope to a waymarked path junction and turn left to join a sandy track. Keep left at the fork and follow the track as it bends sharply to the right.

5 On reaching the road, turn left and, when it bends left by some gates, go straight on along the bridleway towards Kennels Dairy. Keep to the left of the outbuildings and stable blocks and walk ahead to several galvanised gates. Continue on the path and when it reaches a field gateway, go through the gate to the right of it, following the path as it runs just inside the woodland.

WHERE TO EAT AND DRINK

Midhurst has several pubs and hotels – among them the Angel in North Street. This extended Tudor coaching inn has a brasserie, set lunches through the week and light snacks in the more informal surroundings of the bar. The Coffee Pot in Knockhundred Row and Ye Olde Tea Shoppe in North Street all offer tea, coffee and lunches.

6 Continue along to the junction, forming part of the outward leg of the walk, turn right and retrace your steps to the bridge. Avoid the path on the left, running along to South Pond, and veer over to the right to rejoin the river bank. Keep going until you reach a footpath on the left, leading up to the ruins of St Ann's Hill. Follow the path beside the Rother, heading for a kissing gate. Turn left and make for a bridge which provides access to Cowdray House. After visiting the house, go straight ahead along the causeway path to the car park.

WHAT TO LOOK OUT FOR

South Pond is one of Midhurst's most popular attractions. Donated to the town by Lord Cowdray in 1957, the pond is part of a tributary of the Rother. Mute swans, Canada geese and mallards can be seen here. A path running alongside South Pond was opened in 1977 to mark the Queen's Silver Jubilee.

Black Down – Green Sussex Fading into Blue

Follow in the footsteps of a distinguished Victorian Poet Laureate on this gloriously wooded, high-level walk in the county's north-west corner.

DISTANCE *4.5 miles (7.2km)* **MINIMUM TIME** *2hrs*

ASCENT/GRADIENT *315ft (95m)* ▲▲▲ **LEVEL OF DIFFICULTY** +++

PATHS *Woodland paths and tracks, some minor roads*

LANDSCAPE *Wooded hills on Sussex/Surrey Border*

SUGGESTED MAP *OS Explorer 133 Haslemere & Petersfield*

START / FINISH *Grid reference: SU 922306*

DOG FRIENDLINESS *Off lead away from car park and roads*

PARKING *Free car park off Tennyson's Lane (by National Trust sign for Blackdown), near Aldworth House to the south-east of Haslemere*

PUBLIC TOILETS *Fernhurst (on Walk 44)*

Situated close to the Sussex border with Surrey, Black Down lies in some of the loveliest countryside in southern England. At 917ft (280m), this prominent, pine-clad summit is the highest point in the county, yet for some reason it has never achieved the popular status of other high Sussex landmarks such as Devil's Dyke, Ditchling Beacon or Ashdown Forest. Part of a plateau of nearly 500 acres (202ha), Black Down is owned and cared for by the National Trust.

Birds and Bees

It was the Victorians who made it a popular local destination for walkers and naturalists. Writers and artists loved it too, and parts of Black Down remain much the same now as they were around the end of the 19th century when young ladies walked here in groups, the botanists among them admiring the plants and wild flowers.

One man in particular gave Black Down his personal stamp of approval – Alfred, Lord Tennyson. The Poet Laureate built his second home here in 1868, living at Aldworth House for the last 24 years of his life. Ever the patriot, it is said he laid the foundation stone for his new home on 23rd April – St George's Day and William Shakespeare's birthday.

Tennyson was greatly inspired by the beauty and solitude of the area, so much so that he was moved to write these words in 'Lines to a Friend':

You came, and look'd, and loved the view
Long known and loved by me,
Green Sussex fading into blue
With one grey glimpse of sea.

Dark Landscape

Black Down is part of the range of sandstone hills which is enclosed by the bowl-shaped perimeter of the North and South Downs. Historic artefacts found in this area indicate there was human activity here as early as the middle Stone Age, 6000 BC. Although the area has been referred to as south-east England's 'Black Country', Black Down's name comes from the firs which rise out of a dark, heathery landscape, and not from the iron industry which once flourished around here. Some of the most ancient tracks in Sussex cut across this hill and the area was once a haunt of smugglers who may have used a cave here to hide their contraband, en route to London from the south coast.

Beacon Site

Not surprisingly, Black Down was chosen as a beacon site, one of a chain to warn London of the threat of invasion on the south coast. The coming of the Spanish Armada in July 1588 was relayed via the beacon here, which would have been lit on a position high up, overlooking the Sussex Weald. This superb walk explores Black Down and its hidden corners. Not only does it guide you to one of the loveliest viewpoints in Sussex, but it allows you to picture its most distinguished resident, Alfred, Lord Tennyson, strolling this glorious plateau and savouring its views.

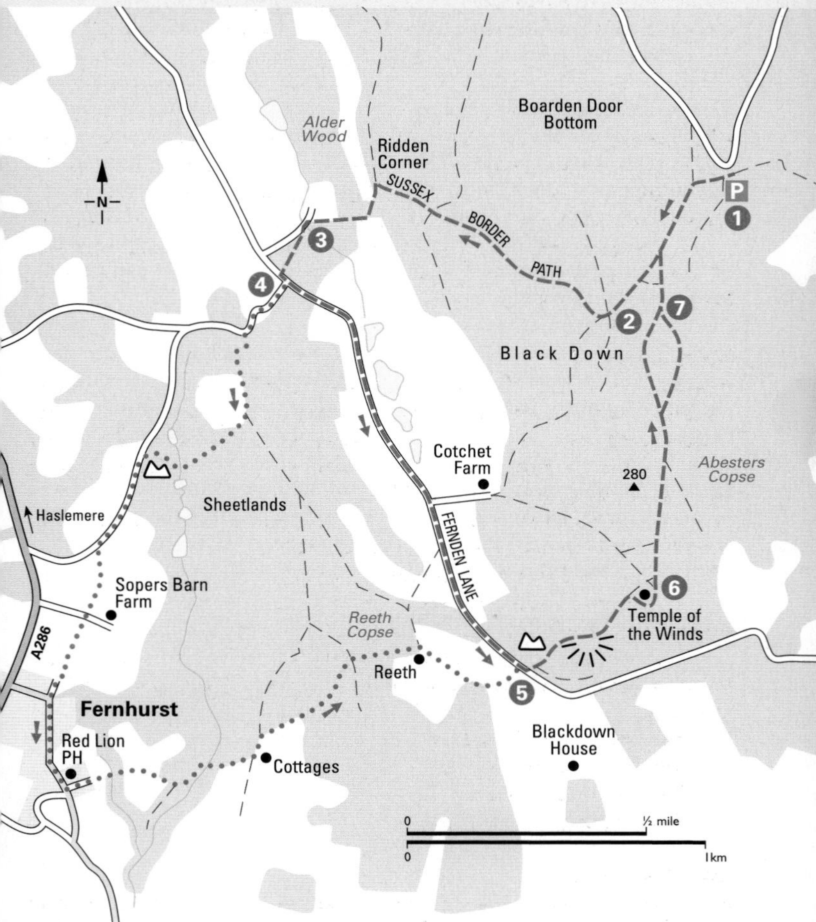

WALK 43 DIRECTIONS

1 Turn left out of the car park and immediately left again on a rising path to the right of the National Trust sign. Keep left at the junction, then swing right at the fork and keep right just after a pond on the right, on the Sussex Border Path and Serpent Trail.

2 Turn right at a complex junction of paths. Keep left at the fork, still on the Sussex Border Path, and pass over a crossroads and through a gate. Veer left just beyond it at the fork and drop down to some rhododendron bushes. Turn sharp left here through a gate and follow the path through a tunnel of trees.

3 Bear left at a drive by a house and when, after a few paces, it curves right, go straight on to the right of a pond through the trees to join the road.

4 Turn left towards the entrance to Sheetlands. Avoid the turning and follow the lane for about a mile (1.6km), passing the entrance to Cotchet Farm on the left. Continue walking along Fernden Lane.

5 Make for a signposted bridleway on the left and after a few paces you reach a National Trust sign. Keep left here and follow the sunken path as it climbs between trees, steeply in places. On the higher ground, follow the path as it winds pleasantly between bracken and silver birch. Fork right past a seat which takes advantage of a magnificent view, partly obscured by trees. Keep the seat and the view on your right and walk along the level curved stone seat at what is known as the Temple of the Winds.

WHILE YOU'RE THERE

The views from the Temple of the Winds are outstanding. Tennyson's old summerhouse stood near the memorial seat at the Temple of the Winds.

6 Do not retrace your steps but take the path running up behind the seat, very soon keeping right and right again at a T-junction. Avoid a path running off sharp right and then a flight of steps and veer left or right at the next signposted fork: both paths soon merge again.

7 Continue ahead and veer right at the next fork. Keep ahead at the next junction, now following part of the Sussex Border Path again. Veer to the right at the fork, still following the long distance trail, and head for the road by the entrance to the car park.

WHAT TO LOOK OUT FOR

Black Down's plateau was once an extensive heath created by grazing and managed as common pasture with bracken cut and gathered for bedding. Thousands of years of grazing sustained our heathlands, but since 1950 nearly half of it has been lost. Before grazing stopped, much of the site consisted of gorse and heathland plant. Later, Scots pine, birch and rhododendron began to grow. The main summit area is dominated by heather and bell heather, with a variety of wetland plants including cross-leaved heath, round-leaved sundew and common and hare's tail cotton grasses. Pine woodland is prolific here, with rowan, birch, gorse, bramble and bilberry. Birds include nuthatch, woodcock, nightjar, linnet and yellowhammer.

Fernhurst's Iron Industry

A longer version of Walk 43 visits the old centre of the Wealden iron industry.

See map and information panel for Walk 43

DISTANCE *6 miles (9.7km)* MINIMUM TIME *3hrs*

ASCENT/GRADIENT *480ft (146m)* ▲▲▲ LEVEL OF DIFFICULTY +++

PATHS *Mixture of woodland and farmland, 4 stiles*

DOG FRIENDLINESS *Near private houses, signs request dogs be on lead*

WALK 44 DIRECTIONS (Walk 43 option)

To extend Walk 44 to visit Fernhurst, once an important village at the centre of the Wealden iron industry, and perhaps have lunch at the Red Lion, turn right at the sign for Sheetlands at Point 4. Follow the tarmac drive through the trees down to a bridleway sign.

Go left up the bank, veering right at the top, and keep to the path as it runs above the drive. Pass above houses and turn right, just after a thatched house, by a waymarker post. Descend an enclosed path, which bends left at the bottom and immediately right by a pond and climbs quite steeply.

Turn left at a signposted T-junction and then follow the driveway past an ornate lamp standard. Turn left on a signposted path, along a line of trees and over stiles. Cross over a driveway and take the path opposite, heading towards Fernhurst. Join a tarmac drive, turn left at the road and then walk through the village to the Red Lion overlooking the spacious green.

On leaving the inn, turn immediately left and follow the tarmac drive, which soon begins an unmade woodland track and later veers right over a stream. Turn left by a wooden barn and cottages and veer right at the next waymarked fork.

Now begin a moderate ascent through the trees. Cross a wide track and continue the climb up through the woodland. Keep right by a house called Reeth. The track bends round to the left and runs up to a junction with a minor road. Turn right, rejoin Walk 43 and follow Points 5, 6 and 7 back to the car park.

WHERE TO EAT AND DRINK

The Red Lion at Fernhurst occupies a lovely position overlooking the village green. On warm summer days, there's nothing to beat sitting outside this 500-year-old building and enjoying its picturesque setting. There's a good range of beers and a varied menu. Bar meals are served all week and the restaurant is open every day.

WALK 45

On the Trundle Trail Above Goodwood

Fine views of sprawling Sussex landscape dominate this remote downland walk which begins beneath the massive ramparts of an ancient hill-fort.

DISTANCE *5 miles (8km)* MINIMUM TIME *2hrs*

ASCENT/GRADIENT *550ft (167m)* ▲▲▲ LEVEL OF DIFFICULTY +++

PATHS *Downland paths, bridleways and tracks. Includes a section of Goodwood Lavant Valley Cycle Route*

LANDSCAPE *Open downland and farmland*

SUGGESTED MAP *OS Explorer 120 Chichester, South Harting & Selsey*

START / FINISH *Grid reference: SZ 873108*

DOG FRIENDLINESS *Long stretches of track where dogs can run free. Keep under control on village roads and patches of farmland*

PARKING *Free parking at Seven Points, Goodwood Country Park (closes at dusk)*

PUBLIC TOILETS *None on route*

WALK 45 DIRECTIONS

Before starting this spectacular walk, make your way up to the obvious path towards the masts and explore the ramparts of The Trundle for an unforgettable view of the Sussex countryside. On the far side of this impressive fortified hilltop, Goodwood Racecourse suddenly looms into view, catching you completely by surprise. The gleaming grandstand and the racecourse's natural amphitheatre setting create a stunning picture. The Trundle, made up of a ditch, dyke and banks, stands 675ft (206m) above sea level and began life as a Neolithic enclosure. Iron Age people later occupied the site and during the Middle Ages, a chapel stood here. Later still, a windmill crowned the summit which was adorned with eight masts during the Second World War.

Head back down to the car park, and turn left downhill on a stony track, heading south towards Chichester and East Lavant. There are glorious views immediately, with the scene dominated by a vast patchwork of fields and hedgerows, and the distant spire of Chichester Cathedral acting as a useful directional landmark. This track is part of a popular cycle route, so look out for cyclists who come beetling up behind you, leaving clouds of dust in their wake on a summer's day. Your walk may also be accompanied by the drone of light aircraft overhead as planes take off and land at nearby Goodwood

WHILE YOU'RE THERE

Have a look round East Lavant and visit the Church of St Mary's. The village lies on the River Lavant, a winter bourne which has been known to dry up for years at a time. The river, which rises near East Dean, passes through Chichester to reach Chichester Harbour.

aerodrome. Continue on the track and, at length, trees, bushes and margins of underbrush obscure the fine views in places.

After 1.5 miles (2.4km) and on reaching the village of East Lavant, turn right and walk along the main street. Pass the Royal Oak and the parish church and cross the bridge over the weed-choked River Lavant. Veer right just beyond it into Sheepwash Lane and pause for a moment or two to study the simple war memorial at the corner of the road. Farmers once washed their sheep in the river here – hence the name.

Follow Sheepwash Lane, bearing right over a brick bridge after 70yds (64m) at the sign for Staple House Farm to follow the bridleway. When the track bends right, go straight on, heading north. The bridleway divides into two parallel paths at one point, but your choice of route doesn't really matter as they all unite further on. Keep forward in the same direction, avoiding a left turn towards some waterworks. The path becomes enclosed by trees and scrub before reaching a gate. The surroundings are once again open and exposed, with the walk keeping to the right-hand side of the boundary fence.

WHAT TO LOOK OUT FOR

Keep an eye out for ravens and honey buzzards on this walk, flying high over The Trundle. The honey buzzard, which nests occasionally in large woods with open glades in the south of England and has narrower wings and a longer tail than other buzzards, has been seen in nearby Westdean Woods Nature Reserve, as have a pair of ravens, distinguished by their heavy shaggy head and massive beak.

WHERE TO EAT AND DRINK

The Royal Oak at East Lavant is ideally placed, although it is more of a restaurant than a pub, it has a small bar and a terrace and a full menu is available. Children and dogs are allowed inside. You might find an ice cream van at Seven Points.

Continue to a gate and 25yds (23m) beyond it you arrive at a blue bridleway waymark.

Veer half right at this point, following the outline of the path as it runs diagonally across the grassy slope. The path reaches a gate in the line of trees, and on a warm day this seems an obvious choice for a five-minute breather. Looking back, there are fine downland views stretching to Kingley Vale on the horizon, with the A286 threading its way across the landscape. The well-wooded country to the right encloses the village of West Dean.

Pass through the gate and follow the path between fields, the spire of Chichester Cathedral seen over to the right, reaching skyward. Wild poppies grow in the field-edges here, adding an extra dash of colour. A large house with sash windows and a slate roof looms into view ahead as you approach the end of the walk. Continue forward past the house and return to the car park.

Espying Chichester's Spire

A fascinating walk combining the ancient treasures of a cathedral city with the delights of the adjacent countryside.

DISTANCE *4.5 miles (7.2km)* MINIMUM TIME *2hrs*
ASCENT/GRADIENT *Negligible* ▲▲▲ LEVEL OF DIFFICULTY +++
PATHS *Urban walkways, tow path and field paths, 2 stiles*
LANDSCAPE *Mixture of city streets and open countryside*
SUGGESTED MAP *OS Explorer 120 Chichester, South Harting & Selsey*
START / FINISH *Grid reference: SZ 857044*
DOG FRIENDLINESS *On lead in Chichester and farmland. Off lead by canal*
PARKING *Fee-paying car park in Avenue de Chartres*
PUBLIC TOILETS *At car park and elsewhere in Chichester*

A stroll through the quaint streets of Chichester is the only way to appreciate all that this small but very beautiful cathedral city has to offer – and it certainly has an abundance of riches. Chichester's origins date back as far as the late Iron Age, and it was settled by the Romans in about AD 200. They built the walls, which can still be clearly identified. During the Middle Ages the city witnessed the building of the great cathedral and its precincts. Later, in the boom years of the 18th century, Chichester really came into its own when wealthy merchants, engaged in the shipping industry and the corn trade, began to build many of the fine houses and civic buildings you see today.

Heart of the City

From the car park it is only a matter of minutes before you find yourself right at the heart of Chichester. Make the cathedral your first port of call. This is the focal point of the city, the Mother Church of the Diocese of Chichester. The spire, a notable local landmark, collapsed in 1861 and was rebuilt under the supervision of Sir George Gilbert Scott who was also responsible for St Pancras station and the Albert Memorial in London. Ranging from Norman to Perpendicular in style, this magnificent building includes the site of a shrine to St Richard, Bishop of Chichester in the 13th century, tapestries by John Piper and Romanesque stone carvings. Another memorable feature is Graham Sutherland's painting, which depicts Christ appearing to St Mary Magdalen on the first Easter morning.

From the cathedral the walk heads down West Street to the intricately decorated Market Cross, built at the beginning of the 16th century and considered to be one of the finest of its kind in the country. It was Bishop Story who made a gift of the cross to the city. He also endowed the Prebendal School in West Street. Situated at the hub of the Roman street plan and distinguished by its flying buttresses, the cross was built to provide shelter for traders who came to Chichester to sell their wares. Make your way up North Street to the Council House, built in 1731 and famous for its huge stone lion and Roman stone. The Latin inscription records the dedication of a Roman temple to Neptune and Minerva. From here it's an easy stroll south to the Pallants, a compact network of narrow streets and elegant houses.

Leave the city now, by following the Chichester section of the Portsmouth and Arundel Canal out into the countryside and south to the village of Hunston. Buildings change and cities continue to evolve, but Chichester's most famous landmark, the elegant spire of its cathedral, remains in view for part of this pleasant walk out and back along the canal.

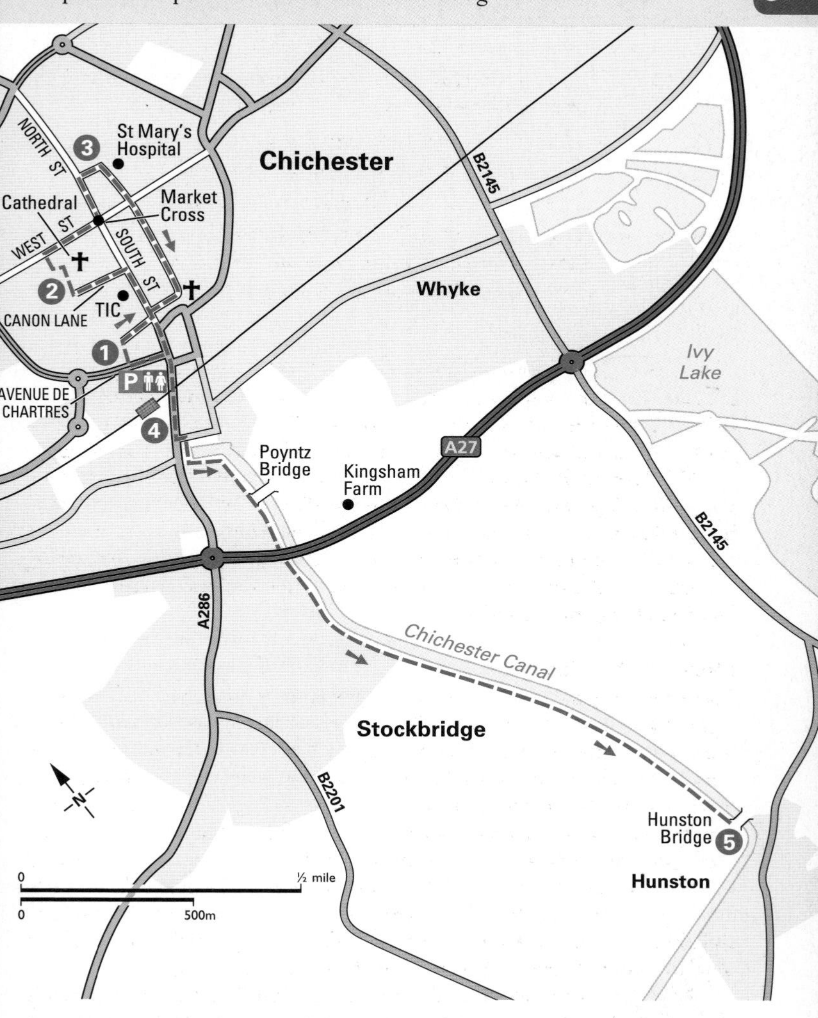

WALK 46 DIRECTIONS

1 On leaving the car park, cross the footbridge over the Avenue de Chartres and head towards Chichester city centre. Turn right at the city map and then left into South Street. Bear left through an archway leading into Canon Lane, just beyond the tourist information centre. Turn right into St Richard's Walk and approach the magnificent Chichester Cathedral.

2 Swing left at the cloisters, then left again to keep the stone wall on your left. Make for the West Door and pass the Bell Tower to reach West Street. Bear right here. Across the road is a converted church, now a pub. The north face of Chichester Cathedral is clearly seen as you head along West Street. On reaching the Market Cross, turn left into North Street and bear right immediately beyond the historic many-arched, red brick Council House into Lion Street.

WHILE YOU'RE THERE

Enjoy a trip on the tree-lined Chichester Canal. It's part of the Portsmouth and Arundel Canal, built to link with other rivers and navigations to form an inland waterway between London and Portsmouth. Designed by John Rennie and opened in 1822, the canal acted as a through route until 1855 and the Chichester stretch was built to take ships.

3 Walk along to St Martin's Square and opposite you at this point is St Mary's Hospital. Turn right and pass the Hole in the Wall pub to reach East Street. Glance to the left and you can pick out the Corn Exchange. Go straight over into North Pallant and walk along to Pallant House Gallery, one of England's finest collections of modern art. Head straight on into South Pallant and follow the road round to the right, passing Christ Church on the left. Turn left at the next junction, make for the traffic lights and continue south into Southgate.

WHERE TO EAT AND DRINK

As well as inns and hotels, of which there are many to choose from in Chichester, there is Clinchs Salad House near the Avenue de Chartres car park and Bishop Bell Rooms, close to the cathedral. The Spotted Cow at Hunston includes a good snack menu as well as more substantial dishes.

4 Cross the railway at Chichester station and then swing left to reach the canal basin. Follow the tow path around the right side of the basin to Poyntz Bridge, dated 1820, and continue to the next bridge which carries the A27 Chichester bypass. Keep going as far as the next footbridge and follow the path to the road. Confusingly this bridge is labelled Poyntz Bridge on OS maps.

5 Reach a wooden bridge at Hunston Bridge and retrace your steps along the canal to the car park in Chichester, enjoying views of Chichester Cathedral's splendid spire on the way back.

WHAT TO LOOK OUT FOR

In addition to the remains of the Roman city walls, there is St Mary's Hospital of the Blessed Virgin Mary in St Martin's Square, founded between 1158 and 1170. Originally a hospital it later became almshouses and is one of Chichester's most historic buildings. Visitors are welcome and can make an appointment with the guide. In the nearby Pallants is Pallant House, built by Henry Peckham, a Chichester wine merchant, in 1712. The house is Queen Anne style and each room reflects a particular period of its history.

Right: Spire of Chichester Cathedral against a blue sky (Walk 46)

West Itchenor – Harbour Sails and Trails

Chichester Harbour's plentiful wildlife and colourful yachting activity form the backdrop to this fascinating waterside walk.

DISTANCE *3.5 miles (5.7km)* **MINIMUM TIME** *1hr 30min*

ASCENT/GRADIENT *Negligible* ▲▲▲ **LEVEL OF DIFFICULTY** +++

PATHS *Shoreline, field tracks and paths, 1 stile*

LANDSCAPE *Open farmland and coastal scenery*

SUGGESTED MAP *OS Explorer 120 Chichester, South Harting & Selsey*

START / FINISH *Grid reference: SU 797013*

DOG FRIENDLINESS *Waterside paths are ideal for dogs but keep under control on stretches of open farmland and on short section of road. Dogs permitted on harbour water tour*

PARKING *Large pay-and-display car park in West Itchenor*

PUBLIC TOILETS *West Itchenor*

Weekend sailors flock to Chichester's vast natural harbour, making it one of the most popular attractions on the south coast. The harbour has about 50 miles (81km) of shoreline and 17 miles (28km) of navigable channel, though there is almost no commercial traffic. The Romans cast an approving eye over this impressive stretch of water and established a military base and harbour at nearby Fishbourne after the Claudian invasion of Britain in AD 43. Charles II had a fondness for the area too and kept a yacht here.

Boat Building Legacy

Situated at the confluence of the Bosham and Chichester channels of the estuary is the sailing village of Itchenor, with its main street of picturesque houses and cottages running down to the waterfront. Originally named Icenor, this small settlement started life as a remote, sparsely populated community, but by the 18th century it had begun to play a vital role in the shipbuilding industry. Small warships were built here by the merchants of Chichester, though in later years shipbuilding ceased altogether and any trace of its previous prosperity disappeared beneath the houses and the harbour mud. However, the modern age of leisure and recreation has seen a revival in boat building and yachting, and today Itchenor is once again bustling with boat yards, sailors and chandlers.

Important Tidal Habitat

But there is much more to Chichester Harbour than sailing. Take a stroll along the harbour edge and you will find there is much to capture the attention. With its intertidal habitats, the harbour is a haven for plant life and wildlife. Wading birds such as curlew, redshank and dunlin can be seen using their differently shaped bills to extract food from the ecologically rich mudflats and terns may be spotted plunging to catch fish. Plants include sea lavender and glasswort, and many of them are able to resist flooding and

Left: Dawn over Chichester Harbour (Walk 47)

changing saltiness. Salt marsh is one of the typical habitats of Chichester Harbour and the plants which make up the marsh grow in different places according to how often they are flooded.

Stand on the hard at West Itchenor and you can look across the water towards neighbouring Bosham, pronounced 'Bozzum'. Better still, take the ferry over there and explore the delights of this picturesque harbour village. It was from here that Harold left for Normandy before the Norman Conquest of 1066. 'The sea creek, the green field, the grey church,' wrote Tennyson and this sums up perfectly the charm of this unspoilt corner of Sussex. Take a little time to have a look at the Church of the Holy Trinity and its Saxon tower base while you're there.

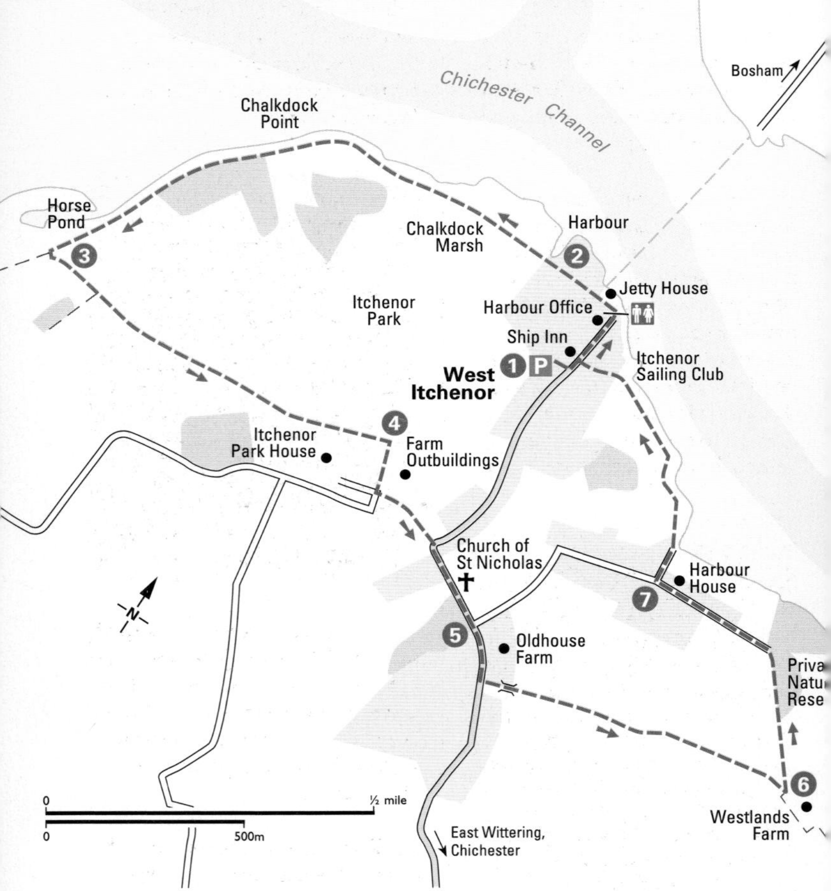

WALK 47 DIRECTIONS

1 From the car park walk along to the road and bear left, heading towards the harbour front. Pass the Ship Inn and make your way down to the water's edge. Look for the harbour office and the toilets and follow the footpath to the left of Jetty House.

2 Cut between hedging and fencing to reach a boat yard and then continue ahead on the clear

WHERE TO EAT AND DRINK

The Ship Inn at West Itchenor dates back to 1803 and was largely rebuilt after a fire in the 1930s. The spacious interior fills up on summer weekends, but there is a good choice of food. The Chichester Harbour boat trip offers light refreshments and is licensed for drinks.

country path. Keep left at the next junction and shortly the path breaks cover to run by the harbour and its expanses of mudflats. Cross Chalkdock Marsh and continue on the waterside path.

❸ Keep going until you reach a footpath sign. Turn left here by a sturdy old oak tree and follow the path away from the harbour edge, keeping to the right-hand boundary of the field. Cross a stile to join a track on a bend and continue ahead, still maintaining the same direction. Pass Itchenor Park House on the right and approach some farm outbuildings.

WHILE YOU'RE THERE

Enjoy a water tour of Chichester Harbour during the summer months, or go in winter when there are regular trips for birding, accompanied by an expert guide. These tours enable you to appreciate the harbour's treasures at first hand and you can see at close quarters some of the many vessels that use it. There are about 12,000 resident boats, with many visiting yachts from the USA, the Far East and Europe.

❹ Turn right by a brick-and-flint farm outbuilding and follow the path, soon merging with a concrete track. Walk ahead to reach the next junction and turn left by a white gate, down to the road. Bear right here, pass the speed restriction sign and soon you reach the little 13th-century Church of St Nicholas.

❺ Follow the road beyond Oldhouse Farm and then turn left at the footpath sign to cross a footbridge. Keep to the right of several barns and follow the path straight ahead across the field. Pass a line of trees and keep alongside a ditch on the right into the next field. The path follows the hedge line, making for the field corner. Ahead are the buildings of Westlands Farm.

WHAT TO LOOK OUT FOR

Just over half-way round the walk you pass the delightful 13th-century Church of St Nicholas, dedicated to the patron saint of children and seafarers. The little church, which has a lychgate, is usually open and inside there are some fascinating treasures. Changes in the window arrangements were made in the 14th century to provide additional light and there have been a number of alterations and additions over the years.

❻ Turn sharp left by the footpath sign and follow the path across the field. Skirt the woodland, part of a private nature reserve, and veer left at the entrance to the Spinney. Follow the residential drive to Harbour House.

❼ Turn right just beyond it and follow the path along the edge of the harbour. Keep going along here until you reach Itchenor Sailing Club. Bear left and walk up the drive to the road. Opposite you should be the Ship Inn. Turn left to return to the car park.

WALK 48

Views and Yews at Kingley Vale

Discover a magical ancient forest and allow your imagination to run riot on this exhilarating walk high up on the South Downs.

DISTANCE *5 miles (8km)* MINIMUM TIME *2hrs*

ASCENT/GRADIENT *440ft (134m)* ▲▲▲ LEVEL OF DIFFICULTY +++

PATHS *Mostly woodland paths and downland tracks*

LANDSCAPE *Dense woodland and rolling downland*

SUGGESTED MAP *OS Explorer 120 Chichester, South Harting & Selsey*

START / FINISH *Grid reference: SU 814125*

DOG FRIENDLINESS *Under control in Stoughton village. Elsewhere off lead unless signs state otherwise*

PARKING *Free car park at Stoughton Down, 8am until dusk*

PUBLIC TOILETS *None on route*

You might not expect to find the largest yew forest in Europe at the western extremity of the South Downs, but that's exactly where it is. This remote downland landscape, covering more than 200 acres (81ha) is cloaked with 30,000 yew trees. Once a wartime artillery range, Kingley Vale became one of Britain's first nature reserves in 1952. Today, it is managed by Natural England.

Gnarled and Twisted Trunks

Silent, isolated and thankfully inaccessible by car, the grove is a haven for ramblers and naturalists. Our walk skirts the forest but if you have the time to explore, the effort is certainly worthwhile.

The yew is one of our finest trees and can live up to 2,000 years. It is usually a large but squat tree, its branches and dark green needles conspiring to create a dense evergreen canopy which allows little light to filter through to the forest floor. With their deep red trunks, branches and shallow roots twisted into monstrous shapes and gargoyle faces, some of the yews at Kingley Vale are thought to be at least 500 years old.

Even on the sunniest summer's day, the scene amid the tangle of boughs is eerily dark, strange and mystical, like something from the pages of a children's fairy tale. The yew has always featured strongly in folklore and, according to legend, this place was a meeting point for witches who engaged in pagan rites and wove magical spells here. Danes and Druids are also believed to haunt the vale.

Ancient Origins

Various theories about the origin of the forest have been suggested but it is thought that the site marks the spot where a 9th-century battle against the Vikings took place. Some sources suggest the trees were planted here to guide pilgrims travelling across the South Downs to Canterbury. Long before the yews began to grow, Bronze Age kings were buried here, confirmed by various tumuli on the Ordnance Survey map.

The trees may be the dominant feature at Kingley Vale but the grove is teeming with wildlife. The delightful green woodpecker, noted for its distinctive colouring, inhabits the reserve, one of 57 species of breeding bird found here. The bee orchid blooms in June while mountain sheep and wild fallow deer keep the turf short for 200 other species of flower. If you're lucky, you might spot a fox or a kestrel.

Beginning just outside the village of Stoughton, the walk immediately makes for dense woodland before climbing quite steeply to the spectacular viewpoint overlooking Kingley Vale. The reserve, renowned for its ecological importance, covers the southern chalk slopes of 655ft (206m) high Bow Hill and from this high ground the views are tremendous.

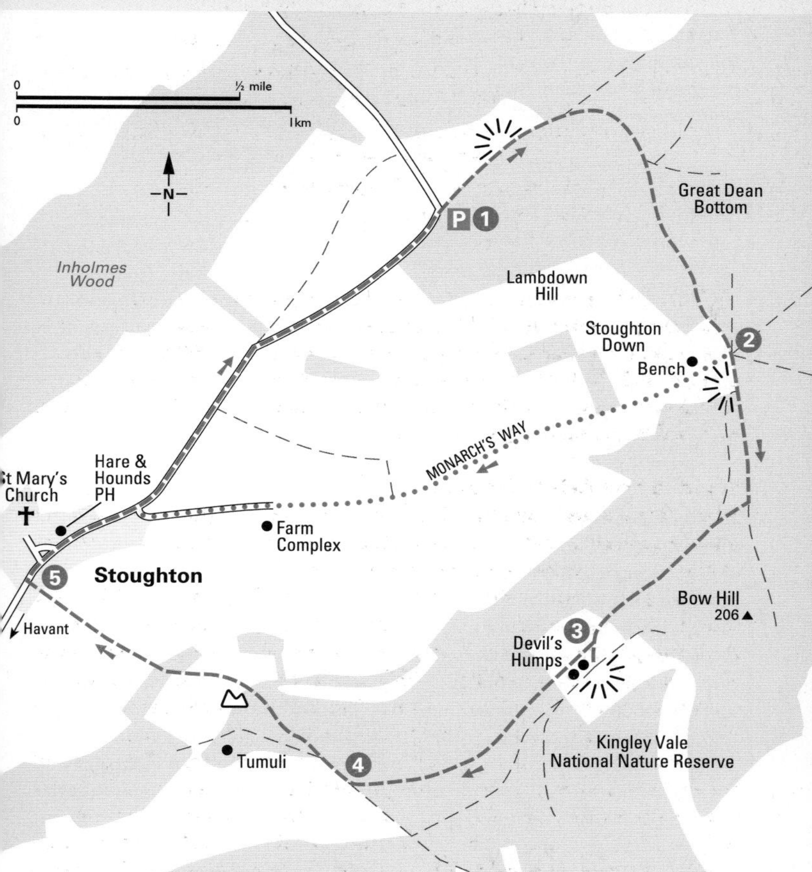

WALK 48 DIRECTIONS

1 Take the bridleway, signposted from the car park entrance, leading away from the road and through a metal barrier, skirting dense woodland. There are striking views on the left over pastoral, well-wooded countryside. Keep right at a fork and follow the stony path as it curves to the right. Veer slightly as signposted right at the next waymarked fork and begin a gradual ascent beneath the boughs of beech and oak trees.

2 Eventually you break cover from the trees at a major junction of waymarked tracks. Go straight on, looking to the right for spectacular views. After 125yds (41m), fork left at the next bridleway sign and join a path running parallel to the track. Cut between trees and keep going for 0.25 mile (400m) until you reach a waymarker post. Fork right here. Keep to the waymarked path as it runs down the slope. Rejoin the stony track, turning left to follow it up the slope towards Bow Hill.

WHILE YOU'RE THERE

Visit Stoughton's 11th-century cruciform church of St Mary. The exterior is barn-like, bulky even, and inside it is unexpectedly spacious. The south transept was converted into a tower in the 14th century, the nave is over 30ft (9m) high and there is a striking Norman arch with a triple layer of roll mouldings.

3 On reaching the Devil's Humps, veer off the path by a sign for Kingley Vale Nature Reserve to enjoy the magnificent vistas across the downland countryside. The view to the north, over remote woodland and downland, is impressive enough, but the panorama to the

WHERE TO EAT AND DRINK

Have a picnic by the Devil's Humps or stop off towards the end of the walk at the Hare and Hounds in Stoughton. This striking flint building dates back to around the 17th century and was originally built as two cottages. Choose from a good snack menu, which includes sandwiches and baguettes, or go for something more substantial such as roast beef salad, lasagne or steak. Everything is cooked on the premises and there are various game dishes in season. There is a terrace in front, and children and dogs are welcome.

south is particularly outstanding. Immediately below you are the trees of Kingley Vale. Return to the nature reserve sign and continue the previous direction along the track, keeping to the right of the Devil's Hump and reentering the forest.

4 Turn right at the next main junction and follow the bridle track along the field-edge. On the left are glimpses of Chichester Harbour, with its complex network of watery channels and sprawling mudflats, and the Isle of Wight beyond. Pass several ancient burial tumuli and then descend through an area of mixed woodland. Keep going until you reach the road, turn right and walk through the pleasant village of Stoughton.

5 Pass the entrance to St Mary's Church on the left, followed by the Hare and Hounds pub. Continue through the village and on the right is the Monarch's Way. Follow the road out of Stoughton, all the way to the left-hand bend where you'll see the entrance to the car park on Stoughton Down on the right.

Stoughton and the Monarch's Way

A shorter walk follows the Monarch's Way recreational trail and still takes in some classic downland scenery.

See map and information panel for Walk 48

DISTANCE *3.5 miles (5.7km)* MINIMUM TIME *1hr 30min*
ASCENT/GRADIENT *334ft (102m)* ▲▲▲ LEVEL OF DIFFICULTY +++

WALK 49 DIRECTIONS (Walk 48 option)

If you don't want to make the climb up to Kingley Vale, or haven't got the time, you can take a short cut to Stoughton, following the route of the Monarch's Way, a 61-mile (1,030km) trail following the escape route of Charles II after the Battle of Worcester in 1651. Though a little less dramatic than the main Walk 48, this shorter alternative still captures the essence of the beautiful wooded South Downs country.

WHAT TO LOOK OUT FOR

Various Bronze Age barrows (burial mounds), known as the Devil's Humps, can be seen up on Bow Hill. There are several legends on the South Downs concerning the Devil. This one suggests that anyone who runs round the humps six times will experience a sighting! As you approach the village of Stoughton on the main walk, look for a memorial stone on the right of the path. It was here in this field, in November 1940, that a Polish pilot officer, based at nearby RAF Tangmere, died when his Hurricane crashed following aerial combat with a German ME109. The memorial is sometimes strewn with poppies and other flowers.

Follow the instructions for Walk 48 from the car park at Stoughton Down as far as the major junction at Point ❷. Turn right here and follow the long distance trail over Stoughton Down, down towards the village. On the right-hand side, just along here, is a nicely placed wooden bench seat.

Follow the bridleway until it branches off to the right and go straight ahead on the waymarked public footpath. Follow the unsurfaced farm road to some substantial outbuildings for cattle, then continue along to the farm complex proper. On reaching the surfaced road, turn right and go directly back to the car park. Alternatively, if time allows, bear left here and walk along to the 11th-century church.

Wide Horizons at West Wittering

Enjoy the salty tang of the sea on this coastal walk by the entrance to Chichester Harbour.

DISTANCE *3.5 miles (5.7km)* **MINIMUM TIME** *1hr 30min*

ASCENT/GRADIENT *Negligible* ▲▲▲ **LEVEL OF DIFFICULTY** +++

PATHS *Beach and water-side paths, road and private drives*

LANDSCAPE *Wide views, natural tidal inlet*

SUGGESTED MAP *OS Explorer 120 Chichester, South Harting & Selsey*

START / FINISH *Grid reference: SZ 772978*

DOG FRIENDLINESS *Off lead on harbour-side paths. On lead in West Wittering and beach*

PARKING *Large fee-paying car park at West Wittering beach*

PUBLIC TOILETS *West Wittering beach and village*

WALK 50 DIRECTIONS

The seaside community of West Wittering is a genteel place, tucked away from the rest of Sussex on a peninsula at the mouth of Chichester Harbour. Despite the hordes of summer visitors who flock to the beach, it retains a dignified air, evoking distant memories of how small seaside towns used to be. The village evolved mainly during the first half of the 20th century, though some elderly residents recall this stretch of coast before it became fashionable, when open fields extended to the superb beach, providing a natural playground for children.

This scenic walk begins by the beach at West Wittering. Follow the drive through the extensive car park, and join the parallel shore path at the earliest opportunity. Pass a row of charming beach huts and a toilet block on the right. Continue ahead towards the mouth of Chichester Harbour, with Hayling Island seen on the far side. Make for the East Head National Trust information board.

Explore East Head and then return to this point. Follow the path along the edge of Chichester Harbour, pass a seat and look to the right for a glimpse of the tower at Cakeham Manor. Continue to Snow Hill, the name given to the part of West Wittering more or less between the church and Chichester Harbour. Though disputed many times over the years, this might be where the Romans landed when

WHERE TO EAT AND DRINK

There are various seaside refreshments available at West Wittering beach, while the Old House at Home in the centre of the village offers a good range of snacks and meals – try the roast of the day or the local fresh fish. Baguettes, sandwiches and jacket potatoes are also available, as are hot pot, various pies and liver and bacon.

WHAT TO LOOK OUT FOR

Cakeham Manor, originally a grand palace belonging to the Bishops of Chichester, lies close to the route of the walk, between West Wittering and neighbouring East Wittering. Its most prominent feature is the tall, distinctive tower which was added to the house in the 16th century and can be clearly seen rising above this flat landscape. The rest of Cakeham Manor dates from around 1800. Neither the house nor the tower are open to the public.

they came to Britain. This site was chosen as the setting for some coastguard cottages, mainly as a precaution against smuggling.

Pass a footpath on the right and keep going along the harbour edge. Cross a slipway to a seat and ignore another path running off to the right. At this point the walk suddenly turns its back on the neat villas and manicured lawns of West Wittering by heading for open farmland and scrub. Keep on the path, with the harbour and marsh landscape on the left, and eventually it bends right by a seat in memory of Penelope Ann Wallace.

Follow the tree-shaded footpath and turn right at the next footpath sign, where there is a gate. Walk along Ella Nore Lane, passing Ella Nore Farm. On reaching the road, opposite the public conveniences, turn left to the junction and then bear right to walk through West Wittering. Pass the Old House at Home inn and continue along the road ignoring Seaward Drive, a private estate.

As the road bends left, veer over to the right and take Berrybarn Lane, over which runs a bridleway. Walk along the lane and again the tower at Cakeham Manor can be seen just across the fields. On reaching the signs for East Strand and West Strand, go straight on to follow a path between panel fencing and bushes. With the beach ahead, turn right towards East Head and follow the path over the greensward. On the right is a row of striking villas, many of them discreetly screened by trees and hedges. Beyond the villas, swing right through one of several gaps along the hedge to return to the car park.

WHILE YOU'RE THERE

Devise your own walk around East Head at the mouth of Chichester Harbour. This slender spit of sand and shingle dunes has changed dramatically during the last two centuries, influenced by the elements. In November 1963 part of East Head was breached by high spring tides and its future looked uncertain. The following year the dunes were artificially reshaped and stabilised before being handed to the National Trust in 1965. Work to restore this sensitive natural feature of the Sussex coast has continued ever since. Among the large numbers of wintering waders and wildfowl found here are Brent geese, shelduck, redshank and curlew. Visitors are requested to avoid the fragile dunes and follow the duckboard sections of path instead.

Walking in Safety

All these walks are suitable for any reasonably fit person, but less experienced walkers should try the easier walks first. Route finding is usually straightforward, but you will find that an Ordnance Survey map is a useful addition to the route maps and descriptions.

RISKS

Although each walk here has been researched with a view to minimising the risks to the walkers who follow its route, no walk in the countryside can be considered to be completely free from risk. Walking in the outdoors will always require a degree of common sense and judgement to ensure that it is as safe as possible.

- Be particularly careful on cliff paths and in upland terrain, where the consequences of a slip can be very serious.
- Remember to check tidal conditions before walking on the seashore.
- Some sections of route are by, or cross, busy roads. Take care and remember traffic is a danger even on minor country lanes.
- Be careful around farmyard machinery and livestock, especially if you have children with you.
- Be aware of the consequences of changes in the weather and check the forecast before you set out. Carry spare clothing and a torch if you are walking in the winter months. Remember the weather can change very quickly at any time of the year, and in moorland and heathland areas, mist and fog can make route finding much harder. Don't set out in these conditions unless you are confident of your navigation skills in poor visibility. In summer remember to take account of the heat and sun; wear a hat and carry spare water.
- On walks away from centres of population you should carry a whistle and survival bag. If you do have an accident requiring the emergency services, make a note of your position as accurately as possible and dial 999.

COUNTRYSIDE CODE

- Be safe, plan ahead and follow any signs.
- Leave gates and property as you find them.
- Protect plants and animals and take your litter home.
- Keep dogs under close control.
- Consider other people.

For more information visit www.countrysideaccess.gov.uk/things_to_know/countryside_code